THE CHANGING

South Oxford

and South Hinksey

BOOK ONE

Carole Newbigging

Robert Boyd
PUBLICATIONS

Published by
Robert Boyd Publications
260 Colwell Drive
Witney, Oxfordshire OX8 7LW

First published 1998

Copyright © Carole Newbigging and
Robert Boyd Publications

ISBN: 1 899536 27 2

OTHER TITLES IN THE *CHANGING FACES* SERIES

Bladon with Church Hanborough and Long Hanborough
Botley and North Hinksey
Cowley
Cowley: Book Two
Cumnor and Appleton with Farmoor and Eaton
St Clements and East Oxford: Book One
St Clements and East Oxford: Book Two
Eynsham: Book One
Headington: Book One
Headington: Book Two
Jericho: Book One
Littlemore and Sandford
Marston: Book One
Marston: Book Two
North Oxford: Book One
South Oxford and South Hinksey: Book One
Summertown and Cutteslowe
St Ebbes and St Thomas: Book One
St Ebbes and St Thomas: Book Two
Wolvercote with Wytham and Godstow
Woodstock: Book One
Woodstock: Book Two

FORTHCOMING

Bicester: Book One
Cowley: Book Three
Cowley Works
Eynsham: Book Two
Faringdon and District
Jericho: Book Two
North Oxford: Book Two
Oxford City Centre: Book One
Thame
Witney: Book One
West Oxford

Printed and bound in Great Britain at The Alden Press, Oxford

Contents

Cover illustrations

Front cover: Marlborough Road street party 1945

Back cover: Coach outing from Church Street (now
               Vicarage Road), New Hinksey c.1945

Acknowledgements

This book would not have been possible without generous contributions from so many people, not only in allowing the use of their unique and precious photographs, but also in spending time with me putting names to faces and sharing their own fascinating memories. I would like to thank everyone for their most valued input, and would apologise to anyone I have inadvertently omitted from this list.

Mrs E Archer	Miss Edens	Mrs B Phillips
Mrs B Beecham	Mr G Fleet	Mr and Mrs J Phillipson
Mrs Bradbury	Mrs B Gordon	Mr A Randall
Mr A Bowsher	Mr R Haines	Mrs W Rich
Mrs D Burnett	Mrs Harris	Mr and Mrs E Shelton
Mr D Califano	Mrs L Hambridge	Mr J Shepperd
Mr R Chasney	Mrs M Hedges	Mrs Tasker
Mr B Crapper	Miss B Horwood	Mrs B Thompson
Mr K Crozier	Mrs P Livett and family	Mr R Timms
Mr R Crozier	Mr A Martin	Mr and Mrs Tombs
Mrs G Drinkwater	Mrs Middleton	Mr and Mrs T Ward
Mrs D Durham	Mrs F Orchard	Mr C Wheeler

Special thanks are also due to
Mr P Clare of Touchwood Sports for the aerial photographs of Cold Arbour;
Reverend Davies of St John the Evangelist Church in New Hinksey;
St Matthews Church and Parish Centre for permission to quote from memoirs collected for their centenary celebrations;
Mrs J Bowley and New Hinksey School;
The Centre for Oxfordshire Studies;
Jeremys Postcards;
Mr T Morgan of Gillman & Soame for permission to reproduce their 1965 photograph of South Oxford School;
Mr Keith Price and Mr John Chipperfield of Oxford & County Newspapers for their continued support;
Mr Iver Harold for the loan of photographs from his fascinating collection and for permission to quote from his even more fascinating memories;
and finally to my mother, Mrs Pat Young, for her valued support in taking photographs, collecting copies and general running around.
I also acknowledge the extracts and use of various other works, most notably
Paul Marriott, *Street Names Explained*;
Kellys Directories, by permission of Reed Information Service; and
Derek Honey, *An Encyclopaedia of Oxford Pubs, Inns and Taverns*.

I would also like to add that seeking out names to put to photographs such as these, some of which may be many years old, is both fascinating and time-consuming. Every effort is made to ensure correct identification, but the occasional error is inevitable when relying on the frailty of human memory.

Dedication

I was born at 35 Lake Street. This property no longer exists, but I have fond memories of my early years in New Hinksey. The house itself was crowded — housing my grandparents, my parents, my uncle and three young children — a typical two-up two-down, steps down to the scullery and an outside toilet. I recall the enamel bath tub hanging on the back door; the bitter cold of the concrete floor in the scullery; the smell of polish from the front room, which was, of course, only ever used for visitors; the dark evenings crowded round the radio — no TV in those days — while grampy dozed in his chair in the corner; bath nights in front of the fire; and the constant smell of damp clothes and ironing. Compared with modern life, I wonder how my parents managed but we were always well fed, clothed and happy. My fondest memories are of long summer days spent at Hinksey Lakes and I recall the day when I was considered old enough — or was it tall enough — to be allowed the other side of the paddling pool railing and into the 2 ft. 9 in. swimming pool! Among other memories are the ballet lessons I attended in the Community Centre opposite my home; the Sunday School in Chilswell Road; the hours spent by the lake at the bottom of Wytham Street fishing for tadpoles with a jamjar suspended from a piece of string; my time with the Brownies when we met weekly in the hall in Vicarage Road.

My family moved along the Abingdon Road to Pitt Road, now Chatham Road, when I was six years old but my grandparents remained in Lake Street for several more years. My mother had attended New Hinksey School, and my brothers and I spent several years at South Oxford Infant and Junior Schools.

Locating material on South Oxford has allowed me to share these memories with so many people and to appreciate the happy childhood that I had. I therefore dedicate this book to my grandparents, Frank and Dorothy Hignell of 35 Lake Street.

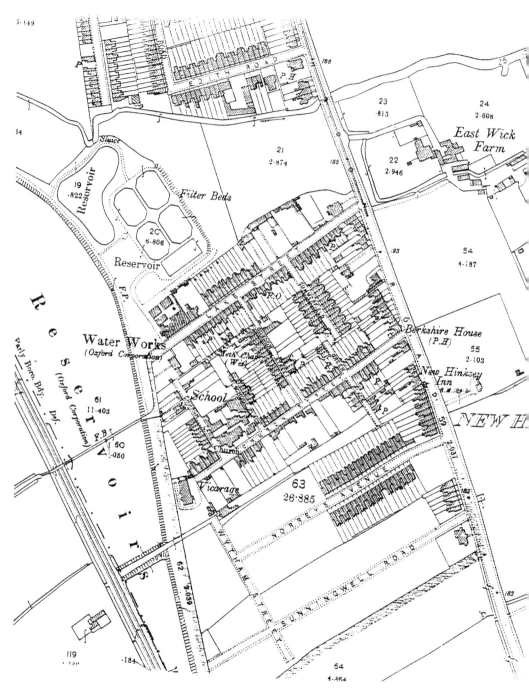

Map showing the early development of New Hinksey. Note the position of the firs
New Hinksey church building in Church Lane, situated on the school's present-day
playground. This small building was demolished in 1905 following the construction o
St John the Evangelist in 1899. Some houses had already been built in Norreys Avenue
but Sunningwell Road and Wytham Street were still to be developed, although it woul
appear that the roads had already been planned.

Map of 1936 showing the development of Cold Harbour, as it was known at this time.

Introduction

'The street which leads from Carfax to Folly Bridge was divided in old days into two portions by South Gate, which stood on the north side of what is now Brewers Street. Although South Gate was removed when Christ Church was built, the street still had two names for the two portions as late as 1750, when Isaac Taylor's map was made; between Carfax and South Gate it was called Fish Street; from South Gate to Folly Bridge it was called Grandpont. The word 'pont' often meant in the Middle Ages an embankment, and not what we mean by a bridge. At Oxford the Great Bridge meant not merely the present Folly Bridge, but the series of arches, more than 40 in number, from the foot of Hinksey Hill to South Gate, together with the embanked road above them. As early as 1282 houses in St Aldates were described as 'super magnum pontem', i.e. 'on Grandpont'. By the 17th century Grandpont had become merely the name of the street.' (Salter, Street Names of Oxford)*

The original Grandpont then was at the southern end of St Aldates, in the area of the present Police Station. The present Grandpont was not really developed until the coming of the railway and the opening up of Oxford's first station in 1879. Much of Grandpont was reclaimed from marshes by the Oxford Building and Investment Company and laid out in a grid pattern on the western side of Abingdon Road, south of Folly Bridge.

Abingdon Road, running south from Folly Bridge, was known, until the 17th century, as the Causey, taking its name from the great Causeway of 40 arches which ran from Folly Bridge to the foot of Hinksey Hill, believed to have been built or renovated by Robert D'Oilly in the 11th century. The Abingdon Road was part of the turnpike that ran from Southampton, Winchester, Newbury, Oxford through to Northampton, and there were two toll gates in the area, one at Folly Bridge, built in 1844, the other further down at Cold Arbour near the Rivermead Hospital.

At the southern end of Abingdon Road is Cold Arbour. 'The name Cold Arbour means 'shelter from the cold', and could indicate a place to rest after a long journey. It was originally a hamlet at the junction of Abingdon Road and Weirs Lane.' (Marriott). The Weirs Lane estate was laid out in the 1930s, so called after the weirs on the old course of the Thames nearby.

To the west of Abingdon Road lies New Hinksey, described in 1902 as 'a modern and populous suburb of Oxford adjoining Grandpont and lying between Abingdon Road on the east side and the Great Western railway on the west. It is in the parish of South Hinksey and in 1889 was transferred from Berkshire to the county of Oxford.' (Kellys Directory). At this time the tram terminus was at Lake Street, opposite Eastwyke Farm, and New Hinksey comprised of only a few streets, Lake Street, Church Street, Sunningwell Road and Norreys Avenue. Further development along the Abingdon Road took place during the 1930s.

The old village of South Hinksey is described in 1902 as 'a parish one mile south from Oxford, from which it is separated by the Isis, over which is a bridge of three arches, and five and a half miles north of Abingdon; in the northern division of the county of Berkshire, . . . and dioceses of Oxford. The Earl of Abingdon is lord of the manor and lay rector, owning the lands formerly belonging to the Abbey. The area is 824 acres of land and 22 of water; and the population of the whole parish in 1891 was 1192, which includes New Hinksey 1011, now transferred to the county of Oxford, and is within Oxford city as extended in 1889.' (Kellys Directory)

South Oxford School

South Oxford School in Thames Street c.1970. The girls were accommodated on the upper floor with their separate entrance on the left of the photograph. The boys were on the ground floor with an entrance to the right of the building. The infant school was a separate building, behind the main building, with its own entrance from Luther Street and its own playground.

South Oxford Council Schools were built in 1910 on a site in St Aldates formerly occupied by the Day Industrial School, established 1879, and the St Michael's Special School. Accommodation was provided for 250 boys, 150 girls and 180 infants; a house nearby in St Aldates was used for handicrafts. In 1948 the schools reorganised as a secondary modern school and a junior mixed school. The school was threatened with closure for many years and was reprieved several times before closing in the late 1970s. The infant school building is currently utilized as a homeless shelter.

South Oxford Girls' School, taken in the playground c.1922/23 includes Miss Walker headmistress, Miss Field, Miss Horn, Miss Beck, Miss Edens, Mona Rowe, Elsie Miller, Dorothy Britain, Winnie Hore, Freda Watts, Phyllis Longford, Rose Shelley, Violet Wright, Nora Carter, Alice Hemmings, May Wilkes, Victoria Ody, Ethel Brown.

The Captain Ball Team c.1929/30. Captain Ball was a game similar to modern day netball but the targets were circles marked on the court. Left to right back row: Doris Carter, Midge Brogden, Freda Williams, Beryl Janaway, Gladys Sims, Gwen Bowells, Rose Townsend. Middle row: Edna Harris, Kathleen Trinder, Dorothy Harris, Joyce Smith, Ivy Nash. Front row: Joan Smith, Edith Moles.

From 1930 Oxford Council Minutes: that certain land at the rear of the houses in Thames Street forming part of the Old Trill Mill Stream, be let to the Education Committee on terms to be agreed, for the extension of the playground for South Oxford Council School.

South Oxford Girls' School Swimming Team of 1935, Winners of the St Aldates Cup and Prizes at the City Police Swimming Sports. Left to right back row: Phyllis Afford, Rachel Robins, Eileen Price, Joyce Bricknall, Margaret Cleaver. Front row: Dorothy Taggart, Edith Wyatt, Winnie Oliver.

The South Oxford school football team c.1949, taken in the playground. Left to right back row: Brian Wintle, headmaster Archie Howells, Bob Edmunds, Ron Osman, Brian Spriggs, Ken Hambridge, sports master Mr Allison. Front row: Brian Smith, Brian Thorn, Bob Gray, Peter Parker, John Shepperd.

South Oxford Boys' School 1938/9. Right-hand side from front to back: Walter Scragg, Harry Robinson, −, Charlie Sallis. Next row: Alan Bowsher, Dennis Broad, −, −, −. '*I remember Mr Howells, the headmaster, also Mr Simpson, Mr Kirby and Mr Blanchard.*'

South Oxford Girls' School outing to Wytham c.1940. Included are Bertha Butler, − Whittington?, Beryl Wootton, June Sloper, Sybil Richings, Marion Palmer, Sheila Watts, Maureen Howard, Anne Clarke, June Butcher, − Canning, Joy Collins, Joan Newell, Rita Long, Dot Butler.

A senior school sports coaching weekend at Bisham Abbey in 1951 includes Mrs Arthurs, Enid Cottrell, Pat Ashmall, Ray Westall, – Butler, Roy Shirley, Miss Hill, June Walton, – Walters, Whitticker, Mick Butler, Marion Palmer, Pete Busby, Pete Cattle, John Cairns, – Hearn, Horace Kelley, Coysh Busby, Ron Budge, Mick Stockford.

The main entrances to South Oxford school were in Thames Street, and along an alley in St Aldates. A back entrance was in Luther Street, which lead to the Infants School situated at the rear of the main school buildings.

South Oxford School 1965. Left to right back row: Steven Smith, Philip Hearne, –, –, Michael Wharton, Tony Jackson, Tony Pomroy, –, Jill Wells, –, Pat Sheridan, Barbara Zippenfinic, Ann Whip, Roger Bolton, Stephen Bailey, Stephen Rowbottom, Henry –, Paul Longford, –, 'Butch' Alder, Peter Jones, David Cheal, –, John Bailey, Susan Berry, Linda Buck. Next row: John Lambourne, –, –, Jackie Hodgkins, Ruth Parker, Linda Pomroy, Julie Roberts, Joy Robinson, –, Peter Harris, Gerald Plumstead, Zena Clarke, Wendy –, Sebina Barrett, Pauline Simms, Gloria Howkins, –, Pauline–, John Hewer, Mick Griffin, Doraine Cross, Christine Gardner, Lorraine Hill, Susan Ostick, – Barrett, Shirley Clark. Next row: Nigel Pugh, –, Roy Cooke, Clive Sherbourne, Christopher Cheal, Paul Palmer, Stephen French, Paul Dawson, Graham Honey, David Dewrey, Brian French, Valerie Bucket, Marlene Zippenfinic, Susan Benham, Julie Gibbons, Paul Trafford, –, –, Soane Lal, Kelvin Harris, Kevin Churchhouse, Stephen Morgan, Lynnette Gilders, –, Brian Lashley, John King, David Witherwick, – Justice. Next row: Allan Whipp, Philip Cooper, Tyrone Roberts, –, Susan Pomroy, Sally Smith, Hilary White, Linda Berry, John Waters, Christine Bailey, Glenis Morgan, Wendy Roberts, Harpinder –, Lorraine Edwards, –, –, –, Paul Adams, Peter Regen, Keith Fisher, David Harris, Clive Robinson, Linda Ellis, –, –, Eileen –, Jean Parker. Next row: Keith Quinell, Eddie Moss, John Horne, Penelope Putman, Sonia Dixon, Hazel Butler, Linda Wharton, John Goodgame, –, –, Les Walls, Philip Tanner, Peter Risk, Ian Coates, –, Graham Jakeman, Paul Adams, Charles Beesley, Tim Dunkley, Peter Strange, Cindy-Lou Elleston, Janet Butler, Christine Sackley. Next row: –, Alan Jenkins, John Coles, Paul Reeves, Mick Weekes, –, Susan Wright, Caroline Drewitt, Peter Wood, Peter Holloway, Pauline Walls, Shirley Kent, Pauline Buck, Christopher Rossiter, Gary Ledger, Andrew Clarke, Julie Oliver, Linda Shelton, Lynne Ward, Martin Sheridan, David Arnold, Janet Butler, –, Patsy Sheridan. Front row: Tony Baker, Terry Jeakings, Steven Honey, Simone Peck, Timothy Sherman, Lynda Ostick, Mr Withers, Mr Kelly, Mr Cooke, Mr Flew, Mr Banton, Headmaster, Mrs Ferriss, Mrs Faulkner, Mrs Clayton, Mrs Couling, Mrs Martin, Secretary, Mr McGregor, Mr Bignall, Penny Dennet, Ann Simms, –, Michael Malony, Christopher Chewings, Terry Newport. (Reproduced by permission of Gillman & Soame.)

South Oxford school trip on 9 April 1963 when 35 children were taken to Riva del Garda in Italy. This was the first continental trip organised by the school for children aged 11 to 15, who were accompanied by the headmaster and his wife, Mr and Mrs D Banton, and teachers Miss Melrose, Mr Flew and Miss Boone.

In September 1978 the school celebrated yet another reprieve from closure of the Middle School, although the Nursery School had already been closed. The school finally closed in July 1981.

Teachers at South Oxford School included Mr Howells, Mr Kirby, Mr Simpson, Mr Blanchard, Miss Benson, Miss Cooper, Mr Clements, Mr Alison. Head of the infant school during the 1950s and 1960s was Miss Wiggle, assisted by Miss Williams and Mr Denton.

Map showing the Wharf area alongside Folly Bridge and the Grandpont development to the west of Abingdon Road.

The Wharf

Baltic Wharf in 1925. The firm of Bassons, on the left, still received regular boatloads of timber from the London Docks, while narrow boats from the Oxford Canal brought coal to the gasworks opposite and collected waste products from the manufacture of town gas. Bassons originally occupied premises in St Aldates, known as the City Saw Mills. *... they stand, for the greater part, well back from the street, but have a portion of their frontage facing St Aldates, with an entrance for carts and other vehicles therefrom. In the rear is a large yard which is surrounded with the various buildings occupied by the firm. The steam joinery is equipped with all the latest steam plant and machinery; and here the various processes of production are carried out with a remarkable amount of precision and neatness. Near this the saw mill is situated, and contains numerous band and frame saws, which quickly reduce the logs to planks of any desired thickness. Messrs. Basson and Co are the only timber merchants in Oxford who have their own steam mills and steam joinery, and who therefore occupy a most important position in their trade.* (*Views and Reviews of Oxford,* 1897). Dolton Bournes & Dolton were a later company of timber importers with an established business along Baltic Wharf. The site was developed during the 1980s and Pembroke College's new quad, the Sir Geoffrey Arthur Building, was built 1987–1990.

Remnants of the boat yards along the Thames.

A view to the west from Folly Bridge. Cobden Crescent is on the left of the photograph. This crescent was named c.1886 after Richard Cobden (1804–1865), British Liberal Politician and champion of the Oxford Building and Investment Company who were responsible for much of the development in Grandpont.

Mr W J I North carried on his business as a brewer of 'Non-Alcoholic Hop Bitter Beer and Stout, and Pure Home Brewed Ginger Beer, and Manufacturer of Non-Alcoholic Wines, Cordials, and Fruit Syrup, and Mineral Water' at 1, 3, 5, 7 and 9 Cobden Crescent.

North's original premises at 1 and 3 Cobden Crescent.

'... the demand for home brewed ginger beer, cordials, syrups, and mineral waters, is very large and progressive, and for the most recent addition to the productive resources of the city is the new and well appointed factory at 1 and 3 Cobden Crescent, Grandpont. This is the head-quarters of the business of Mr W J I North, who established himself there eighteen months ago. Mr North's family have been connected with the trade for three generations. The new venture at Oxford has met with a most encouraging measure of support, and the sale of his goods has, we are assured, been going up by leaps and bounds.

The factory is regarded as the most complete and modernly equipped of its kind in the city, or for many miles round. The building is of solid two storeyed construction, and is a striking feature on the 'Up-the-River' side of Folly Bridge. It has an inclined concrete floor, and the drainage and sanitary arrangements may be regarded as the most perfect of their kind. The factory is supplied with a steam plant of the most recent pattern, capable of output of over 1000 dozens of bottles per day of mineral waters.' (Views and Reviews of Oxford, 1897)

A view of the tow path and the back of Isis Street taken during the 1960s from the landing stage at Folly Bridge. The old Norths Mineral Water Factory, seen on the left hand side, was occupied as a Coca Cola factory.

Demolition of the old mineral water factory in June 1970.

Old Salters boathouses in Brooke Street.

The Oar and Scull Works in Jubilee Terrace along the towpath.

Jubilee Terrace, named c.1888, commemorates Queen Victoria's Golden Jubilee of 1887.

COBDEN CRES. (Grandpont), from 2 Buckingham st. to 41 Marlborough rd.

SOUTH SIDE.

1, 3, 5, 7 & 9 **NORTH & CO.LIMITED**, mineral water manufacturers. Tel. No. 2323

3 Webb Geo. M. S
5 North & Co. Ltd. mineral water manufrs. (office)
  Walsalls Conduits Ltd. mfng. electrcl. engnrs
11 Harris Chas. Jeffery
13 Huckings Geo. Stanley
15 Cordery Rd
17 Green Horace Regnld
19 Coles Chas
21 Greenwood George

NORTH SIDE.

..... *here is Jubilee ter* ......

2 Harris George & Son, boat builders. See advertisement
4 Ponting Hy. Edwd
6 Short Geo. Wm
8 Smith Sidney O

MARLBOROUGH RD. (Grandpont), from River Isis.
[No thoroughfare.]

EAST SIDE.

3 Watts Miss
5 Alder Arth. Alfd
7 Beckley Harold
9 Marchetti Chas
11 Oliver Fredk. Wm
13 Gilder Mrs
15 Pitcher Thos. Arth
17 Williams Thomas
19 King Mrs. Martha, certified midwife
21 Watts William
23 Cox Chas. Hy
25 Hudson Albt. Geo
27 Castle Gilbert
29 Weller Bert
31 Boyles Mrs
33 Mold Alfd. Jas
35 Hansen Wm
37 Watts Thos
... *here is Cobden cres* ...
41 Chandler Hy
43 Wiltshire Hy
45 Dingle Miss
47 Washbrook Sidney T. O
49 Wright John
51 Perks Jsph
53 Baker Nathaniel
55 Waldron John William
57 Buy Fredk. Wm

59 Trafford Mrs. A. M
...... *here is Western rd* ......
St. MATTHEW'S CHURCH
... *here is Whitehouse rd* ...
  St. Matthew's Infants' Day School
77 Hedge Wltr
79 Holloway Arth. Jn
81 Whiting Gilbt. Geo
83 Collett Ernest Alfred
85 Willis Alfd. Ernest
87 Greenaway Frank
89 Gealer Wltr
91 Ingram Mrs. L
93 Dixon Mrs. E
95 Bricknell William
97 East Mrs
99 Richmond Mrs
101 Cooper Philip Arth. W
103 Bates Joseph William
105 Smith Charles Henry
107 Warne Jesse Albert
109 Walsh Albt. Edwd
111 Butterfield Mrs
113 Clifford Fredk. Thomas
115 Castell Albt. Victor
117 Hedges Edwin Wm
119 Reeves Benj. Augustus
121 Wells Wm
123 Price William
125 Willis Frederick
127 Bayliss Samuel Charles
129 Comley Mrs. F
131 Ward Jas

......*here is Newton rd* .....

135 Clifford Miss
137 Beesley William Hy
139 Rosser Lewis Robert
141 Payne Mrs
143 Crapper Victor Albt
145 Burden Ernest Harry
147 Marriott James Albert William
149 Mills Sidney H
151 Jones Hy. Arth
153 Pickford Mrs
155 Penny Eli
157 Dean Henry
159 Breakspear Jas. Alex
161 Tritton Albert George
163 Piddington Jsph. E
165 Edney Arthur
167 Wintle Geo. Edwd

169 Hitchcox Sydney W
.... *here is Deans Ham Recreation Ground* ......

WEST SIDE.

2 Hayes Mrs
8 Bossom Norman
10 Perry Mrs
12 Weller Ernest Edwd
  Basson T. & Son Ltd. timber mers. (Baltic wharf)
18 Hearn Misses
20 Dowsing William
22 Goode Arth. Bates
24 Trinder William Thomas
26 Stevens Mrs. D
28 Bateman Wm. Jas
30 Simpson William Joseph
34 Green Edwd
38 Trafford Harry
40 Fogden Mrs
40A Oxford Cabinet Co. (The), cabnt. mkrs
42 Edmonds Jn
44 Hunt Thomas
46 Ryman Frederick
48 Grundy Albt. Fredk
50 Kilbee Henry
52 Morris Jas. Wltr
54 Hore Charles
56 Skuce Geo. Edmnd
58 Lewin Albt
60 Hearn Regnld
62 Cripps George
64 Silvester Geo. Elon
66 Taylor Cyril Wilfred, genl. shop & post office
68 Trinder Mark Ernest
70 Coggins Ernest
72 Marson Mrs
74 Druett Mrs. A
76 Richmond Harry Thos
78 Steptoe Hy. Jsph
80 Collett Wm
84 Collins Mrs
86 Huish Mrs. E
88 Trafford Wm. H
90 Robins Chas. Fredk
92 Bossom Wilfred
94 Olney Rupert F
96 Rennie Harold Chas
98 McGowan Jn
100 Shepperd Wm. Stanley
102 Oxley Mrs
104 Shepherd Peter Thomas

106 Martin Ernest H
108 Betts Mrs
110 Walker Stuart
112 Stickley Thomas Edwin
114 Slatter Mrs
116 Timms Albt. Edwd
118 Sheard Vernon
122 Margetts Daniel N
132 Day William
134 Pollard Saml
136 Hookham Arth. Wm
138 Brown Benj
140 Coleman Frederick Hy
142 Archer Charles James
144 Bridger Miss H. N
146 Tombs Arth. Chas
148 Bonner Albert Edward
150 Lloyd Albert Edwd
152 Jeffrey Christopher Fdk
154 Barham Chas. Edwd
156 Hadland Wm. T
158 Reeves Jsph
160 Hadland Ernest
162 Level Mrs. R
164 Ash Arth
166 Rainbow Miss M. E
168 Nutt Albt. Edwd
170 Braithwaite Bertie
172 Green John
174 Phipps Mrs
176 Grain Rt. Geo
178 Knight James
180 Tredwell Gilbt. Sidney
186 Bowell Mrs. Jessie M. grocer
188 Stevens Cecil Herbert
190 Samsworth George Thos
192 Andrews Chas. Herbt
194 Janaway Harold James
196 Savin William Thomas
198 Little Arth
200 Pledge Charles
202 Breakspear Albt
204 Deeley James Albert
206 Dunn Sidney John
208 Hiles Mrs. Florence, shopkpr
210 Gardner Mrs
212 Sloper Mrs
214 Springer Chas. Edwd
216 Weatherhead Miss
218 McBride Reguld. Jsph
220 Collett Wilfred F. F
222 Wiggins Charles
224 Franklin Albt. Edwd
226 Hicks Mrs

Extracts from Kelly's Directory 1937 (by permission of Reed Information Service).

Grandpont

Abingdon Road looking south from Folly Bridge. White Horse Road is on the right-hand side. Note the tram lines running down the centre of the road.

Grandpont is named after the causeway of stone bridges built by Robert d'Oilly in the 11th century. However, the original Grandpont was at the southern end of St Aldates, in the area of the present Police Station. In 1279 that Grandpont was listed as having only 62 houses and the present Grandpont was not really developed until the coming of the railway and the opening up of Oxford's first station by Folly Bridge in 1879. Much of it was reclaimed from the marshes by the Oxford Building and Investment Company and laid out in a grid pattern to the western side of the Abingdon Road. (Honey)

In 1902 Kelly's Directory describes Grandpont, an area of some 315 acres, as 'to the south of Oxford and along the Abingdon Road; a tithing of the parish of St Aldates, from which it is separated by the Isis, but is connected with the city by Folly bridge, and is bounded by the parish of South Hinksey. Formerly in the county of Berkshire, by Art. iv of the City of Oxford Order 1889 under the Local Government Act 1888, it was transferred to Oxfordshire and is included within the extended city of Oxford.

View of Marlborough Road from the west. Marlborough Road was named c.1880, and it is believed was previously known as Archer Street. At the back of Marlborough Road are several fields, including Deans Ham at the bottom of Marlborough Road and Welshman's Mead further along, towards the river. In the smaller field next to Deans Ham was a large hoarding sign, facing the railway, which read 'Archer & Cowley Shipping and Removal'. The company of Archer & Cowley may have owned or leased this field, and the approach to it may have been known as Archer Street.

The church of St Matthews in Marlborough Road was originally a chapel of ease for St Aldates parish. Designed by Messrs Christopher and White of London in 15th century gothic style, and built by Messrs Symm and Co for £7,965, the foundation stone was laid by the Bishop of Oxford on Saturday 21 June 1890. St Matthews became a separate parish in 1913. In 1933 a mission church of St Lukes, in Canning Crescent, was established to serve the growing population of Cold Arbour, which was in the parish of St Matthew's.

The third annual report from St Matthews church, in 1894, stated that *'There are in the district, including Cold Arbour, at the present date 1750 people located in 393 houses. The apparent diminution in the population is accounted for by the fact that a portion of Grandpont, comprising 42 houses and 180 people, is not counted this year as last, it having been discovered after diligent search that it belongs to another parish. Of the total given, some 460 are children under twelve years of age; 370 are Nonconformists and Dissenters; 190 are known as workers in connection with, or regular attendants of other churches. During the year some 32 houses have been built; 15 are in course of erection, and 8 are unoccupied. The population of the district is almost exclusively working class.'*

In 1931 the population of Grandpont, including St Luke's in Cold Arbour, was 3,317.

St Matthews Choir c.1938. Left to right front row: Peter Samsworth, Granville Fleet, Albert Greenwood, John Harrison, Charles Gibbons, Victor Mayor. Second row: Doris Hine, Harold Reading (small boy), Mr Cyril Samsworth, Mr Rosser, Reverend Hine, Reverend Stather-Hunt, Tommy Edwards organist, Douglas Pearce, Ralph Martin, Herbie Gibbons (small boy), Minnie Watts. Third row: W Breakspear?, Alan Rosser. Fourth row: Bert Timms, Len Franklin, Alan Martin, Geoff Mead. Fifth row: Jack Woods, Cyril Mash, Len Simms, Cecil Shelley. Back row: Gilbert Hitchcock, Les Shepherd, Toby Watts. *'The Choir under the direction of Tommy Edwards was well balanced with Boys, Men and Women. The boys were regularly replaced as their voices broke.'* (St Matthews Parish Centre)

St Matthews Church outing, possibly to Weymouth c.1932. Left to right back row: Betty Brooks, Mrs Brooks, Mrs Harold, Miss Cis Fowler, Mrs Dean. Front row: Aubrey Brooks, Aubrey Harold, Zena Brooks, Ivor Harold, Violet Dean, –. Charlie Dean in front. *'The Deans used to live in Marlborough Road, and at Christmas their house was festooned with decorations – you could not see the ceiling.'*

1914—1918

P C Ash	F C S Little	H F Saunders
W G Ash	H H Little	H S Scragg
A Belcher	A J Lucas	G E L Simpson
J Benson	A C Margetts	A E Smith
E W Brooks	E R Marriott	E S Smith
C Castle	W J Merry	J W Smith
R C Cherrill	R J Norgrove	R W Stevens
A H Cobb	A E Oliver	H Tallett
C J Collett	P Palmer	A G Taylor
P Collinson	A G Phipps	T H S Townsend
B C Coppock	W J Phipps	C G Tyrrell
G H Cox	A W Pitcher	F H L Upfold
A T Dolley	J A Prestidge	V W Venables
C V Drury	F J E Pullen	A J Walcroft
L G Edens	W J Rennie	A C Wallis
W Hicks	F Revell	E Webb
E Hook	A E Reynolds	A L Whiteley
W J Ingram	L P Reynolds	E Whiting
J Irwin	W E Richardson	F Woodley
E L Jago	R V Robinson	W Woodley
W R King	H Rough	A Wright
E J Little	L J Ryman	E J Wright

1939-1945

K Ayres	R G Collins	W P Hedges
H Bannister	B Comeley	A Martin
E G Boswell	C Daft	F Molyneux
E Bowles	D Drew	G E Morrison
L Boyles	J C English	H J Sawyer
R Breakspear	E Finch	L Shepperd
R Buttram-Gardener	M Goddard	F Thompson
K Cole	H H Hacksley	R Williams

St Matthews War Memorial.

On the wall near the door at the west end of the south wall is a large brass mounted on wood and surmounted with a wooden crown. This commemorates those who died in the 1914—18 war. On a pillar opposite this is an inconspicuous brass tablet listing the fallen of the 1939—45 war.

The Reverend David Keith Stather-Hunt, vicar of St Matthews, 1929–1975. He was also prison chaplain at Oxford Prison from 1929, becoming full time on his retirement from St Matthews, at which time he was a Canon. During the Second World War, Mr Hunt entered the Forces as a chaplain.

Stather-Hunt, in relaxed mood, in 1931 on a church outing to Bablockhythe.

After becoming a separate parish our first vicar was Reverend W A Williamson, who was very fond of children. Reverend William Chadwick followed, a very sincere devout man who made a lasting impression on my young life. His wife, a very lively person, had the gift of inspiring one with her enthusiasm. Under her leadership the Sunday School grew rapidly and her lively ability at the piano drew a spontaneous response from the children. The Sunday School Teachers were frequently invited to tea on Sunday afternoons at the Vicarage, and the Vicar entertained us with 'Parsons Jokes' told with his solemn ability. Once a week we met for a sewing session to make things for the Annual Church Sale of Work held in the Church School, previously it had been held in the Randolph Hotel. The Stalls were gay with bunting, and filled with a variety of goods, the centre attraction being the Plant and Flower Stall provided by the Turner family of Cold Arbour. Their son, Andrew, is well remembered for his jolly personality when delivering milk round Grandpont – not in bottles in those days. (St Matthews Parish Centre)

Charlie Crapper in the garden of 106 Marlborough Road. Mr Crapper was a coal merchant and also owned a grocers shop on the corner of Western Road and Marlborough Road. Next to the shop were bakery premises, the Grandpont Bakery at 59 Western Road. When Charlie died c1937 the bakery premises were taken over by a former employee, by the name of Backs. *'We used to buy one half of a quarten of dough (about 4lb) take it home in a cloth, Mum would knead it and put it in a tin, then take it back to the bakery for baking.'* Part of the bakery premises was leased in 1948 by Arthur Carter who established the Grandpont Creamery, making and selling ice cream.

Charlie Crapper c.1920 outside the yard in Marlborough Road. *'At the bottom of the yard was the stable and up above a room where he cut chaff for the horses. Us Boys used to gather in that room and help cut the chaff.'*

rapper's Yard showing its proximity to the church. The yard was sold, c.1992, to the church for the building and development of St Matthews Parish Centre.

n the left is Reg Sloper of 212 Marlborough Road c.1920 when he was a delivery boy r J Sainsbury. On the right is Sid Hitchcock of 169 Marlborough Road c.1950. Mr itchcock was employed at Twinings on the Banbury Road. His wife was related to izabeth Anstey, Lady Nuffield. In 1902 the property was occupied by Charles Anstey, florist.

Mr and Mrs Fowler and Clara Fowler of 90 Chilswell Road. He was a builder, former of Eynsham and St Ebbes, and the family kept a general shop and sold coal.

'We lived in Chilswell Road, with Mrs Fowler. An old friend of our landlady, bor and brought up in Grandpont, well remembered before our houses were built, when brook ran at the bottom of our gardens, there were quite a few willow trees. He als recalled when, on the right-hand side of Kineton Road, was a meadow with cows an goats grazing on it.' (St Matthews Parish Centre). *Kineton Road was named afte Kineton in Gloucestershire, and means Royal Manor. Spelt Cyngtun in 969, Quintor in 1086 and Kinetin in 1230, the street was named in 1902.* (Marriott)

Edith Road looking towards Chilswell Road. The Grandpont Arms public house is the left-hand side of Edith Road; its landlord in 1902 was Frederick Jefferies. *Edi Road was possibly named after Sister Edith, who died 1898, assistant superior at t Sisterhood of St Thomas across the River Thames. The street was named in 189* (Marriott) The large house in the middle of the photograph is 90 Chilswell Roa formerly occupied by the Fowler family.

group of children at a May Day parade during the 1940s in the grounds of St
atthews School. The church can be seen behind the school wall. St Matthews School
as built on a site in Marlborough Road, on the corner of Whitehouse Road, given by
asenose College, and became the infant school for the whole parish. By 1951 the
emises were out of date and the managers applied for aided status. The school closed
1959 and is now demolished.

St Matthews Parish Magazine 1894: *We are very grateful for the success which
tended the laying of the Memorial Stone of our New Schools. The day was
nfortunately anything but fine, though during the ceremony not a drop of rain fell;
ut there were over 1,500 people present. The Duke of Marlborough performed his
nction in a graceful manner. The Grandpont Church Choir leading the praises.*

In April 1894 it was reported *'that the large field adjoining the Schools (usually
lled Mr Gray's field) has been sold for building, and that we may expect an addition
 upwards of 100 houses within the next couple of years.'*

The Parish Magazine further reports *'The first meeting in the Schools was held on
riday 22 June 1894. After prayer in the playground that God would protect our little
nes from accident, and give them hereafter a place at His right hand, where there is
easure for evermore, the door was reached, and God besought to open the Kingdom
 Heaven to many in that building through the teaching and preaching of the Word of
od. In the cloakroom, we prayed that many might be clothed in the Robe of Christ's
ghteousness; in the lavatory, that souls might be washed in the Blood of the Lamb;
en on to the classrooms and large room, where a meeting was held, composed chiefly
 workers.'*

St Matthews School 1929 Class I. Left to right front row: Stan Samworth, Billy White
– Conley, –, –, –. Middle row: Dorothy Martin, Iver Harold, –, Joan Codd, – Salte
Back row: – Turner, –, John England, Linda Breakspear, –, –. At this time Miss Morle
was headmistress.

St Matthews Infant School 1935/36.

St Matthews Infant School May Queen celebration 1936. Left to right: Avis Bossom, Pamela Brightman, Edmund Drew, Roy Witchall, Betty Martin, Nora Scragg, Peter Juggins, Joan Holland, June Crapper, Beryl Sawyer, Reggie Bateman, Rosemary Turner, Brian Milton, Barbara Batten, Arthur Wright, Peter Samsworth, Brian Oliver, Dianne Oliver May Queen, Alan Rosser, –, Trevor Coles, Jean Bateman, Vernon Ward, Molly Juggins, Eatwell sister (1), Myrtle Martin, Granville Fleet, Eatwell sister (2), Albie Greenwood, Reggie Watts, –, –.

This Marlborough Road street party in 1945 includes Ann Ash, Peter Borebone, Bernard Crapper, June Walton, Mrs Collett and Mrs Butterfield.

Boys' Brigade and Girls' Brigade

The Brigade was an important institution in Grandpont, and had a profound effect on the lives of many young residents. Marjorie Cowley was Leader of The Life Boys from 1929 to 1966, and Officer in Charge of The Junior Section from 1966 1980.

Miss Cowley was a young Sunday School teacher in 1929 when she was asked to play the piano for the meetings of The Life Boys. Soon she was to take the position of Leader. After 51 years of service, she retired as the Leader of the Junior Section of The Boys' Brigade, as it was then called. In 1979 Marjorie was presented with the British Empire Medal for her devoted service.

'In 1929 Reverend David Keith Stather-Hunt was appointed Vicar of St Matthews. A young enthusiastic Boys Brigade Officer, he quickly introduced the Brigade to the parish. The Junior Boys, called The Life Boys, were trained to take their place in the Brigade at the age of 12. Four female Sunday School Teachers were appointed as Leaders. At a later date the Girls' Life Brigade was formed and the Leader of the Girls' Sunday School, Miss Gladys Cowley, was appointed Captain, later becoming Commandant of the Oxfordshire Battalion.

The Life Boys lost their title in 1966 when Brigade Council integrated them into The Boys Brigade as one company, and the sailor hat was replaced by the company hat and a woven badge took the place of the metal Jersey Badge. They were then known as The Junior Section.

The Girls' Brigade, The Boys' Brigade and The Life Boys all held their annual displays in the Oxford Town Hall. These were real highlights for St Matthews and drew crowds of people. By the time the Life Boys became The Junior Section, the cost of hire of the Town Hall was too great and the Display was held in South Oxford School.

The Golden Jubilee of 1st Oxford Boys' Brigade, 19 May 1979, was celebrated by a special display given by the Junior Section, as, owing to the resignation of the founder Captain of the Company through age and ill-health, the Company Section had been forced to close. It was re-formed by Alan Bowsher shortly after the 50th Anniversary Display. The Founder Captain, Reverend D K Stather-Hunt was able to be present at the Display and to play the Leading Roll in the Final Item from his wheelchair. Although very weak he obviously was very pleased to be present with so many of his old Boys and their parents and old members of St Matthews in the audience.' (St Matthews Parish Centre)

The 1st Oxford Boys' Brigade Football XI of 1946 in the grounds of St Matthews Infant School. Left to right back row: Reverend Stather-Hunt, Trevor Coles, John Reading, Don Hicks, Donald Wiltshire, Alan Rosser, Lt Walton. Middle row: Bob Gray, Peter Samsworth, 'Chick' Terry, Edmund Drew, Albie Greenwood. In front: Norman Beesley, Tony Bricknell. Bob Gray was a Schoolboy International and captain of the England team for several years. He died tragically young.

Boys' Brigade 1937 swimming team against Witney. Back, standing: –, –, –, Stather-Hunt, Ken Hearne, Les Shepherd, –, –, Derek Drew, –, –, –, –. Middle, kneeling: Ron King, Eric Chasney and Johnny Strange. Front: –, Alan Bowsher.

The Life Boys c.1945. Left to right back row: −, −, Clive Walker, −, Brian Spriggs, −, Philip Martin. Next row: −, −, Peter Morris, −, −, Howard Redding, −, −, John Gray. Next row: John Shepperd, Terry Walsh, David Holloway, −, −, −, John Cook, −, −, −, Stuart Henry. Seated: Graham Fleet, Harold Redding, Miss Cowley, Mrs Shepperd, Tony Bricknell, Bob Gray. Front row: Ted Gray, − Gibbons, Peter Borbone, −, Ronnie Keegan, −, Ray Timms, Tony Bishop.

The Girls Life Brigade c.1937/38. Left to right back row: Heather Deeley, Dorothy Martin, Winnie Phillips, Mary Franklin, Doreen Harris?, Gladys Knight, Ruth Franklin, Betty Morgan. Next row: Daphne Ward, Cathy Loveridge, Barbara Mash, Stella Cox, Barbara Pain, Barbara Ash, Jean Hewer, Francis Greenwood, −. Next row: Olive Morgan, Betty Bricknell?, Audrey Phillips, Miss Gladys Cowley, Reverend Stather-Hunt, Miss Phipps, Edna Samsworth, Eileen Martin, Barbara Batten. Front row: −, Molly Juggins, −, Alison Martin, Barbara Hewer, Lily Sylvester, Hazel Martin, Jean Bateman, Betty Martin.

The 1st Oxford Company Boys Brigade 1934. Left to right front row: Harry Freighter, John Chandler, Reg Hearn, Charlie Gosling, − Phillips, Eddie Wiggins, Stan Townsend, Freddie Batton, − Morgan. Second row: Ken Hearne, −, Ray Hewer, Aubrey Harold, Ralph Martin, −, Gordon Wheeler, Iver Harold, −, Gilbert Hitchcox, −, 'Titch' −, Frank Eldridge, − Lloyd, Ben Deeley. Third row: John Leverman, Ron Little, − Rosser, −, −, Charlie Dean, Frank Holloway, Aubrey Brooks, − Butler, John Strange, −. Back row: Eric Kitchen (third from right), Roland Breakspear (holding the flag), Stan Famworth (right at the back), Wally King (on left of row).

Winners of the Inter-Company Cross Country Trophy 1935. Left to right back row: Ken Hearn, R Hearn, − Hewer. Front row: − Hornblow, − Taylor, R Morgan.

The 1st Oxford Company Boys Brigade 1946. Left to right back row: Frank Walters, Bob Gray, Don King, Roy Whiting, Gerald Mead, Don Wiltshire, Albert Greenwood, Ralph Walton. Next row: Donald Hicks, Peter Attewell, Terry Miles, –, Leslie Marchant, Keith Bennett, Norman Beesley, Nogger Best, –. Next row: –, Harold Redding, Froggy Morris, –, Richard Elliott, Tony Parsons, Babs Ledger, Trevor Boswell, –, Peter Gee, Dixie Dean, Terry Walsh, –, Alan Shorter, –, –, Toj Wintle. Next row: –, David Coles, R Burtonwood, –, –, Jasper Thorne, Tony Bricknell, Don Cooke, –, Graham Fleet, –, Michael Flegg. Front row: Sid Morris, John Redding, Trevor Coles, Alan Rosser, Alan Bowsher, Mr Ted Walton, Reverend Stather-Hunt, Mr Doug Pearce, Mr Downing, Peter Samsworth, Edmund Drew, Basil Terry, Granville Fleet.

The Girls Life Brigade 1946. Left to right back row: Barbara Mash, Shirley Williams?, Mary Willshaw?, Eileen Bayliss, Grace Martin, Anthea Reading, –, Ethel Whiting, Iris Cooper, Jean McDougall, April Jackson, – Marchant, Sylvia Walker, –, –, Maureen Baskerville?. Next row: Jean Aldridge, Cynthia Wiggins?, Jean Collett, Mavis Coombes, Ruth Martin, Isobel Bull, Pamela Fleet, Irene Ash, Rita Butterfield, Pamela Coleman, –, –, Barbara Scragg?, Marjorie Canning. Next row: Jean Loveridge?, June Crapper, Peggy Bossom, Nora Scraggs, Jean Slatter, Miss Gladys Cowley, Beryl Coleman, Betty Martin, Myrtle Martin, Eleanor Downing, Lily Sylvester. Next row: Judith Harris, Cynthia Baldwin, –, Maureen Aldridge, –, Gillian Martin, –, –, Diana Williams, Anne Ash. Front row: Judy Booty, Brenda Fleet, June Walton, –, Joyce Cooper, Terry Martin, Cora Reading, – Gee, –, –. Miss Gladys Cowley was a leader of the Girls' Sunday School and was appointed Captain of the Girls' Brigade, later becoming Commandant of the Oxfordshire Battalion.

The Grandpont Minors in 1941 on Deans Ham ground. Left to right back row: Charli Dean, Alan Martin, Dennis Brooks, Cyril Mash, Geoff 'Daisy' Mead, Roy Simm David Talboys, Gerald Willis. Front row: – Finch, –, Rex Adams, Eric Hewer, Eri Pilbeam (an evacuee), Peter Turner.

The Grandpont Giants, the cycle speedway team c.1953. Left to right back row: Ton Wirdnam, John Coles, Doug Ward, Gordon Sherman. Front row: Maurice East, Geral Smith, Viv White (mascot), Doug Califano, Jock Sutherland.

The cycle track in Deans Ham field c.1951.

Action shot 1959. Grandpont Giants v. Horspath Wreckers. Left to right: Gerald Chambers (spectator), Kevin Rowlands, Brian Winchester, Pat Souch.

eans Ham Recreation Ground was also home to the South Oxford Football Club, seen ere in 1956. *'That year we won the Oxfordshire Junior Shield and the Oxford City FA's remier and Junior Cups'.* South Oxford were unbeaten for 42 matches — nearly two easons. The players are Gordon Maizey, Bert Timms, Maurice Sampson, Georgie arter, Norman Bricknell, Alf Jefferies, Harry Grain, Ron Osman, Pete Gee, Don Cook, eoff Barrett, Ray Timms, Pat Morris. Also included are Harry Spicer, — Sherman, Mrs Viggins wife of the Chairman, Cynthia Wiggins, Pete Smith, Pete Stedman, Bill rozier, Ken Naughton, Mr and Mrs Lane, Mr Allsworth, John Maizey, Fred Wiggins, hairman, Eddie Wiggins, Dick Bayliss, Haydn Webb, Roland Allsworth, Mr Lloyd.

South Oxford Football Team Second XI, 1954/55 season, winners of the League Cu
Final and League Shield. Left to right back row: — Sutton, — Tutton, —, Dick Ward
Maurice East. Front row: Pete Smith, Mick Butler, John Reed, Gordon Ledwell, Bria
Lait, Brian Lane.

Deans Ham Recreational Ground was opened by the council and was formerly par
of Grandpont Farm, owned by Tuckwells and occupied by farmer Hathaway in th
1930s. It was not a proper farm, but the surrounding land was quarried for gravel an
the area was also known as Tuckwells Meadow. *'I can remember a man used to occup*
a hut at the end of the Rec. I think his name was Butler, but us boys used to call hir
Gramps because of his big white moustache. A footbridge led across the stream to a.
untouched field full of moondaisies and tomthumbs — beautiful it was. I ca
remember both Deans Ham and that field being cut by hand, with a sythe, must hav
taken them about three weeks. There were a fair few frogs around, out of the stream
suppose, and the man cutting the field used to pretend to swallow a small frog — lef
us boys open mouthed! They left the grass to dry and then loaded it onto horse and car
with pitchforks and took it away.

They used to hold carnivals on those meadows — a large stage at the back, wit.
gymnastics and clowns. I remember the Al Fresco Five performing, including Perc
Hewer of Bridwell Square. At night there would be a large fireworks display. They als
had the occasional circus — invariably Lord John Sangers circus (Lord being
Christian name) — and they used to bring the big animals in by rail, unload th
elephants and parade them through the town to advertise the circus. At the corner o
Whitehouse Road there used to be a big tank of water for the elephants and I believ
they also took them down to the river. I don't remember the circus continuing after th
war.' (Harold)

New Hinksey

'he laying of the foundation stone for the new church of St John the Evangelist at New Hinksey. This 1899 photograph includes: Mr Kingerlee builder, Bishop Stubbs, Rev C N Hicks, Canon Bright, Rev W D B Curry vicar of South Hinksey with New Hinksey, Rev I N Bate, Canon B J Kidd, Rev W Scott of Cowley, Canon Clayton of St Mary Magdalen, Rev C A Marcon? curate and Rev Hudson of St Barnabas. The architect, Mr J Ninion Comper, is standing on the right-hand side, just to the right of the upright post.

This new building was to replace the smaller edifice which had been built in 1869 as *a building to serve as a school for six days a week and a church for the seventh. To be built of white brick with stone dressings for the buttresses. The benches on which the children sit in the week day will be moveable, some of them being so constructed as to be convertible into desks for writing.' (Jacksons Oxford Journal, 1869)*

1914—18

Horace Adams	Frederick Greenstreet	Horace Sawyer
Joseph Bayliss	Alexander Hay	Edward Shaw
Joseph Bellinger	Harold Higgins	Albert Smith
Archibald Brocks	Wilfred Higgins	Frederick Soundey
Leslie Brocks	John King	John Soundey
Harry Carter	Herbert Lee	William Speaks
George Chandler	Frederick Mace	Frederick Webb
William Chandler	Charles Martin	Frederick Wharton
Albert Collins	Levi Mitchell	George Williams
George Cox	Percy Palmer	Arthur Woodley
William Donohoe	Reginald Parsons	William Woodley
Thomas Eldridge	Richard Quinion	William Hounslow
James Ferriman		

1939—1945

Peter Atkins	Reginald Collins	William Marriott
Kenneth Ayres	Harold Haynes	Leslie Revell
Charles Bowley	Albert Harris	John Rowley
John Boyle	Henry Kitching	Frederick Taylor
Harold Brown	William Lynes	John Turner
Albert Carr	Donald MacKenzie	Frank Whittington

The War Memorial in the church of St John the Evangelist at New Hinksey in the parish of South Hinksey.

In 1902 New Hinksey was described as 'a modern and populous suburb of Oxford, adjoining Grandpont and lying between Abingdon Road on the east side and the Great Western Railway on the west; in the parish of South Hinksey. In 1889 it was included in the county borough of Oxford and transferred from Berkshire to the county of Oxford. The present church of St John the Evangelist was opened by the Bishop of Reading in 1900. It is built on a site adjoining the vicarage and erected in place of the small edifice which formerly stood between School Place and Church Lane and which was built in 1870. At present (1901) only the western half of the church is built, at a cost of over £6,000, and will seat about 400 persons. The living is a vicarage, in the gift of the Earl of Abingdon, and held since 1891 by the Reverend William D B Curry, MA of Exeter College.' (Kellys Directory by permission of Reed Information Service)

New Hinksey Girls, St John's Church King's Messengers. Back row, left to right: Nancy Coles, —, —. Middle row: Elsie Pitts, —, —, May Blake. Seated in front: Mollie Stimpson, —, —. The girls are on the lawn at the side of the vicarage. Today this is a completely enclosed garden but was formerly a tennis court built by Reverend Lander.

New Hinksey Girls dancing at the Summer Fete. The dancing girl on the right is Trixie Grundy.

Lake Street was so named c.1886 after the nearby Hinksey Lakes. This photograph, looking towards the Abingdon Road, was taken during the floods of 1894. Gordon Street is on the right-hand side. The Crown, seen here on the right-hand side, became a public house in 1871. Its first licensee was William Ward who was followed by Mr Parrott and, in 1890, a member of the old water barge family, George Basson. Mrs Butler was a well loved landlady in the 1950s and the Crown was known locally as 'Butlers'.

An outing from the Crown in 1951, including Frank Hignell, Wally Wale and Bill Exler.

The ladies group, including Pat Hignell, Joan Hands, Joan Allin, Edith Allin, Freda Reed, Mrs Waine, Mrs Honey, Rosemary Moss, Mrs Richardson. Mrs Butler, the landlady, can be seen in both photographs.

An outing from the Crown in Lake Street in 1952. Left to right back row: Mr Trafford, Mrs Trafford, George Allen, Colin Smith, 'Wap' Waine, –, Mrs Smith, Tommy Deacon, Beryl Deacon, Bert Archer, Margaret Hedges, Sid Hook, Edie Exler, Barbara Exler, Edith Archer, Mrs Butler landlady, Mrs Richmond, –, Mrs Summers. Middle row: Susan Hedges, Hazel Hedges. Front row: –, Maureen Exler, Christine Archer, Roger Deacon, –, Bill Exler.

An outing from the Crown in Lake Street c.1953. Left to right standing: Frank Hignell, –, –, –, –, Les Cook, Michael Ward, –, Vi Butler, –, Mr Ward, Bill Exler, –, –, Stan Hignell, Wally Whale, Sid Hook, Stan Hedges, Edgar Coombes. In front: Mr Thick, Tommy Deacon, John Reed.

The Seven Stars, at 30 Lake Street, was first recorded as a public house in 1871. It was built by Morrells who, in 1875, valued it at £177 10s. They charged the tenant, James Leaver, £15 per year rent. Aunt Sally was always popular, and this photograph shows the 1956/57 team with an impressive collection of trophies. Left to right back row: R Howkins, Gordon Barrett, Bert Archer, B Longford, Vic Reed, Len Coterell, B Higgs, D Atkins. Front row: Tommy Deacon, Bill Exler, Bill Fry, Ken Warmington.

The Seven Stars Aunt Sally team of 1958. Left to right standing: Jack Tomkins, Ken Alder, Ken Exler, Bert Archer, Len Cotterill, Wally Wale, Bill Francis. Front row: John Barson, Bill Exler, Frank Spencer.

The Silver Threads Club in the late 1940s met at The Guild, now the South Oxford Community Centre in Lake Street. Front row: −, −, Mrs Buck, Mrs Horwood, Mrs Launchbury −. Back row: −, −, Mrs Bannister, −, −, −, −, Mrs Stickly (third from right), −, Mr Marshall.

Guild outing c.1937, includes Les Shepherd, Tom Lund and Bill Phillips.

The Guild was formed by a committee of six local people who protested about the lack of facilities for the young people of the district. They petitioned every household in Hinksey, Grandpont and the Friars district of St Ebbes. The management of the Water Works at the bottom of Lake Street agreed the use of a hall within the building. The South Ward Oxford Social Guild was officially named by Mrs Horwood, founder member. Facilities included table tennis upstairs, with a snooker room downstairs. The Guild arranged a youth club twice a week and concerts during the war, raising money mainly for the merchant navy.

Steward Street, at the back of Lake Street, in 1951 and a young Tony Lovegrove of Lake Street home on holiday from The Royal Hospital School in Ipswich. Stewart Street leads to Gordon Street, named after General Charles George Gordon who was murdered in Khartoum in 1885. Gordon Street was named c.1886 and was formerly known as Cross Street, named c.1874, or Stround's Buildings.

The Wesleyan Methodist Church, the white building in the middle of the row, in Gordon Street, New Hinksey, opened in 1888 and closed in 1940. During the Second World War it was used as the Civil Defence Club, later becoming the South Oxford Social Club. Stan King is remembered as a long-time steward, and John 'Bubbles' Barson took over after Mr King died.

'There was a chapel where we went to Sunday School. For good attendance you would get a red star on a card, with a full card you were able to go on the outing to the seaside. When war came it was taken over by Duffields to store flour; after the war it was empty for a time, then it was taken over by the Civil Service Club.'

A children's Christmas party in the South Oxford Social Club c.1940.

Members of the South Oxford Social Club outside the University Pavilion on the Abingdon Road, the original home of the Social Club, prior to moving to Gordon Street. Left to right back row: Ken Charlwood, Harry Charlwood, –, –, –, John Charlwood, Mr Senior. Middle row: Christine Hogg of the Duke of Monmouth, Mr Bill Skuce, Bob Sumner, –, Stella Harvey, Ernest East, –, –, George Harris, –. Front row: –, Mrs Read, –, Mrs Andrews, Stan King, –, Mr Andrews, Walter Charlwood.

VE Day party 1945 in the South Oxford Social Club. Group includes Mrs Hedges, Hazel Hedges, Susan Hedges, Joan Allin, Mr Sumners, Rona Skuce, Miss Sumners, Bob Simmons, Hilary Crowther, Pat Palmer.

'Everyone knew Old Jaynie Mathews in the big house at the bottom of Lake Street, opposite the Guild. She was a little woman, always dressed in black and us kids were convinced she was a witch. Another character was Bravo Couling from 3 Lake Street. He owned or leased some fields near the Farriers' Arms in Cold Arbour, known as Bravo Couling's fields.'

Vicarage Road was so called after the old vicarage built near the lake c.1850 and also New Hinksey Vicarage built in 1887 by H W Moore at the west end of the street. It was formerly Church Street and was officially renamed in 1955 to distinguish it from several other Church Streets in Oxford. It was also previously known as St Johns Street after the nearby church, and Post Office Road after the nearby Hinksey Halt where post was collected from the trains.

The Edward VII at 51 Vicarage Road, named after King Edward who reigned between 1901 and 1910, was first recorded in 1893 when it was possibly called the Price of Wales. A large grand building, it had two main bars, one on each side of the central door, and a large rear garden. Once a thriving pub with several darts, Aunt Sally and bar billiards teams, it finally closed in 1991 and is now private accommodation.

The Edward VII Aunt Sally team of 1947. Left to right back row: Jo Johnson, Arthur Coppock, Ernie Hook, George Moss, –, –, Jack Pipkin, Tom Smith, –, Bill Lee, –. Front row: Ken Clarke, Jack Goodenough, Bill Robinson, Ted Parker, Bert Pipkin landlord, Fred 'Sacky' Heritage, Bill –.

The Edward VII Aunt Sally team of 1951, League Champions, Winners of HKO Cup, Pairs and Oxford City FC Supporters' Cup. Left to right: Jack Goodenough vice-captain, Bill Bates, W Robinson, George Bowler, Arthur Coppock, Ken Alder, Jo Howes, Les Shepherd, Sid Sloper, Jim Symmonds landlord. Seated: Ted Parker, catain, Freddie Heritage.

Coach outing c.1945 in Vicarage Road, then Church Street. The Edward VII public house can be seen at the bottom of the road on the left. The building on the extreme left was the Eton Fives Courts, University courts for 'real tennis'. The group includes: John Watkins, Joan Watkins, Colin Smith, Nobby Clarke, Tony Lovegrove, Janet Howkins, Brenda Ward, Chalky Blisset, Mike Shearer, — Gibbs, Christian Horwood, Mr and Mrs Horwood, Barbara Gibbs, Peter Cook, Douglas Ward, Margaret Warmington, Pat Hignell, Mrs Lee, Mrs Coppock, Sylvia Beesley, Arthur Coppock, Lawrence Coppock, Alf Millard, Megan Gardner, Mrs Ward, Mrs Parker, Stan Hignell, Mrs Bunce, Mrs Mullins, Mrs Gibbs, Mr Siggers, Mrs Turner, Mr Charlie Lee, Reg Lee, Bill Lee, Frank Brewster, Mr Parker, Ron Parker, Bob Soundy, Mr Mullins, Michael Ward, Mrs Sumner, Mrs Joyce Smith, Mrs Dorothy Hignell, Mr and Mrs Cook, Elsie Clewley, Alice Hayward, Bill Higgs.

Sunningwell Road was named, in the 1890s, after Sunningwell village, Berkshire. The name means 'valley, hill and spring of Sunna's people' and was spelt Sunnigwellan in AD 811, Sunnugauuille in 821 and Soningeuel in 1086. At the bottom of Sunningwell Road were two shops, Browns on the left and Snelgroves on the right. At one time six policemen lived in the road, including Temple and Goodchild who became Chief Constable of Northampton, and George Shelton.

PC 51 George Shelton of Sunningwell Road on Aldens field during a fete c.1930 leading a donkey ridden by John Harding of Lincoln Road. An *Oxford Mail* photographer offered PC Shelton 'a guinea for you to get on that donkey', an offer which he declined.

Number 42 Sunningwell Road in 1907. Alice Lovegrove with two stepchildren, Dorothy Lovegrove and Augustus Garner Lovegrove. The railings in front of the property were removed during the Second World War for use as scrap metal for the war effort.

Norreys Avenue, much as it appears today but without the obstruction caused by parked cars. The avenue was named in 1893 after Lord Norreys, James Bertie, who was created Earl of Abingdon in 1682. Norreys Avenue would appear to have been built along the line of a lane, called Madams Lane, shown on an Estate Map of 1814.

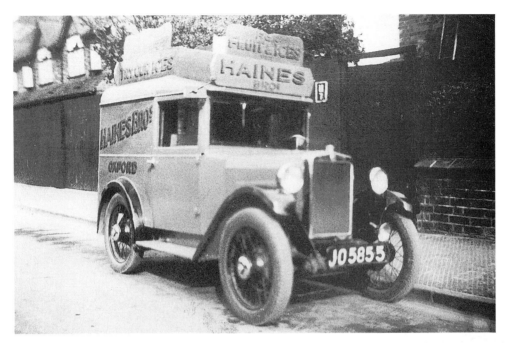

A familiar sight along the Abingdon Road was Haines' van. The first known van, in the early 1930s, was driven by Bernard Haines who named it 'Little Plum'.

The Haines family arrived in Oxford about 1918 from Witney and settled at 69 Norreys Avenue. The family comprised of James Haines (1868–1950) and his wife Emily with children Sadie, Ernest, Bert, Reg, Marjorie, Bernard and Ted. Mr James Haines had a horse and cart from which he sold fish and chips. Shortly after 1927 Bert purchased a shop on the corner of Abingdon Road and Lincoln Road and established a fish and chip shop. These premises are still occupied as such.

A later van, c.1950, parked in Monmouth Road.

The 50th Wedding Anniversary of James and Emily Haines, 28 May 1944, at University Pavilion, Abingdon Road. Left to right back row: Katy Haines, Lilian Haines, Cathleen Haines, Arthur Carter, Jenny Haines, 'Peg' Califano, Eileen Haines. Next row: Bernard Haines with David Haines, youngest son, Albert Haines, Ernest Haines, James Haines, Emily Haines, Sadie Carter, Reg Haines, Marjorie Califano, Ted Haines with baby Sheila, his daughter. Next row: Raymond Haines, Mavis Haines, Ronald Haines, Joan Haines, Margaret Carter, Audrey Carter, Gwen Haines, Douglas Califano, Keith Haines, Yvonne Haines.

Two other sons, Bernard and Reg, were the first in the family to make ice cream at Norreys Avenue. After Reg's marriage, the brothers continued to make ice cream from Reg's home in Wytham Street and sold this, together with fruit, from mobile vans. After going their separate ways, Reg carried on selling from his van, a mobile shop, until he retired. Bert continued the family tradition of ice cream making from the rear of the chip shop, later moving to the Varsity Works in Wytham Street.

Sadie married Arthur Carter and he worked with Bert making ice cream. About 1948 Arthur rented a property in Marlborough Road where he made ice cream. This was the Grandpont Creamery and was sold from Arthur's vans. The family supplied ice cream around the villages in Oxfordshire and at St Giles Fair where Bert had a stall and Reg sold from a three-wheeled tricycle.

South Hinksey Village

A view from John Piers Lane looking towards The Stores taken during the floods of 1960.

South Hinksey is a parish one mile south of Oxford and five and a half miles north of Abingdon. It is in the Northern division of the county of Berkshire and diocese of Oxford. The River Isis, over which there is a bridge of three arches, separates South Hinksey from Oxford. The village retains some houses of the 16th century, and John Piers, Archbishop of York (1589—95) is said to have been born here. There is a Baptist Mission room. The Earl of Abingdon is lord of the manor and lay rector, owning the lands formerly belonging to the Abbey, and is the chief landowner. The area is 824 acres of land and 22 of water; rateable value £3,899; and the population of the whole parish in 1891 was 1,192, which includes New Hinksey 1011, now transferred to the county of Oxford, and is within Oxford city as extended in 1889. (Extracted from Kellys Directory of 1902.)

In early days it used to be known as 'Old Hincksey', spelt with a 'c' in the middle.

The footpath to South Hinksey from New Hinksey, over the 'Devil's Backbone', looking towards the General Eliott public house during the 1930s. Concrete bridges were built after the Second World War. *'On the way to New Hinksey school we boys used to be able to rock those old wooden bridges – almost managed to knock down the one over Hinksey Stream.'*

'The name South Hinksey is Anglo-Saxon in origin, derived from Hengestesieg, meaning Hengest's Island. The village can be approached from Jacob's Ladder, the bridge over the railway, and along an old track called Devil's Backbone or sometimes Devil's Causeway or Hogs Back. To the right can be viewed a row of willow trees, marking the line of the old Green Lane which, prior to 1932, was the only link with North Hinksey Village. In 1932 the by-pass, later the A34, was opened.' (Phillipson)

A letter dated 25 June 1917 sent from a gentleman, George Hinds of London E17, to Henry Taunt, the famous Oxford photographer recalls a tragedy that took place at the General Eliott in the early 1800s. 'The chief figures in the drama were a young man named Taunton, son of Sir Henry Taunton, or was it Thurland?, who lived in the house on the Towpath below Folly Bridge (occupied in my time by Ald Randall); and Ann Morgan, daughter of the landlord of the General Eliott. The incidents as related to me by the members of my mother's family, descendents of the parties concerned, are as follows. Morgan, the landlord, had a handsome daughter being courted by young Taunton, who had promised her marriage. This was known to his family, some members of which, especially his sisters, bitterly opposed it. The girl found herself pregnant and at the same time took a violent dislike to her lover, refusing to have any further relations of any kind, including marriage with him. On the eve of the tragedy Taunton is said to have gone to the General Eliott and after trying in vain to induce the girl to see him, blew out his brains in the garden. Of the girl it remains only to say that she gave birth to a daughter and shortly after left England as a sort of travelling companion to a lady of position. The child was put out to nurse and was educated at this lady's expense. At about eighteen years of age she married Thomas Dolley, senior, of the Dolphin & Anchor, Folly Bridge. The late Wm Dolly was one of the sons of this union.'

A group of regulars outside the General Eliott in the 1930s, including Bert Messenger, the landlord's son, Jack Howkins senior, Jack Howkins junior, 'Brook' Launchbury, 'Mac' McKenzie, Ern Walton?, Dickie Sawyer?. The General Eliott, originally a farm dating from the mid-1700s, was named for the national hero, George Augustus Eliott, who defended Gibraltar against the Spanish and became Governor of Gibraltar in 1775. The Messenger family were landlords for many years.

SOUTH HINKSEY.

Letters arrive through Oxford.
The Parish Council consists of five members; Chairman, Miss W. Toynbee; clerk, R. Hext, 41 Laburnum rd. North Hinksey
Church of St. Laurence; Rev. A. G. Whye M.A. The Vicarage, Vicarage road, New Hinksey, vicar, & surrogate

PRIVATE RESIDENTS.

Ainslie Chas. M. 4 Church close
Aldwinkle Miss, Pin Farm ho
Allsworth Albt. 8 Manor rd
Allsworth Jn. 3 Church close
Amos Jn. 36 Manor rd
Arthur Bernard, 44 Manor rd
Atkins Mrs. D. 11 St. Lawrence rd Stone End, Hinksey hill
Bayliss Geo. 30 Manor rd
Beaver Frank H. The Brambles, Spring copse
Beaverstock Horace, Highway, Hinksey hill
Beesley Ronald A. Bagley Croft lodge, Hinksey hill
Bellhouse Michl. A. H. Woodside, Hinksey hill
Boardman Jn. 32 Manor rd
Booth Mrs. G., Fairfield, Badger la
Boreham Anthony R. St. Michaels, Spring la
Boreham Fredk. Geo. St. Martins, Spring copse
Borrett Mrs. Woodlands, Hinksey hill
Brewerton Gordon W. Bagley croft, Hinksey hill
Bruce Jas. F., M.A. Dellstone, Hinksey hill

Chambers L. G. Thatches, Hinksey hill
Chandler Cyril, 3 Manor rd
Charlett Mrs. 6 St. Lawrence rd
Cook Wltr. J. Orchard cott. Chilswell path
Cooper Graham R. Shepherds close, Hinksey hill
Cooper Mrs. Woodlands, Hinksey hill
Crozier Cyril, 1 Chilswell path
Davies Mrs. N. de G. The Copse, Hinksey hill
Davis Bernard E. The Red ho. Hinksey hill
Farrar Arnold, The Gables, Hinksey hill
Flower Wm. The Lawn, Hinksey hill
Forrest Mrs. Spring copse
Gibbons Mrs. B. 22 Manor rd
Green Roland, 9 Manor rd
Hare Mrs. Pin Farm cott
Harris Mrs. 3 Ivy cotts. Hinksey hill
Herbert Norman C. Corscombe, Hinksey hill
Horton Frank, 7 Church close
Howkins Hy. 1 John Pier's la
Howkins Jn. Manor farm
Howkins Lewis, 2 Church close
Hughes Frank S. 10 Manor rd
Hulbert Frank, 2 Chilswell path
Hulin Peter, The Bungalow, The Copse
Humphreys Gordon F. 48 Manor rd
King Wltr. G. 3 Chilswell path
Kingsbury Arth. Drake ho. Spring copse
Knipe Jsph. H. The Bungalow, Hinksey hill
Leed Jn. E. Beaumont, Hinksey hill
Lewis Fras., Heverlee, Hinksey hill
Litten Stanley, Meadow Sweet, Bettys la
Lonsdale-Cooper Mrs. N. E. Lane end, Hinksey hill
Minns Fredk. Jn. Solway, Badger la

Organ Herbt. V. Charnwood, Hinksey hill
Organ Regnld. J., Roslin, Spring copse
Organ Wm. A. The Firs, Hinksey hill
Palmer Anthony, 46 Manor rd
Parker Geo. 17 Manor rd
Parslow Ernest, 1 Church close
Phipps Ray, Brookside, Bettys la
Rand Cyril, 6 Church close
Ridley Sidney, Broom, Hinksey hill
Robbins B. G., Broombarn, Hinksey hill
Rogers Albt. R., Wayside, Hinksey hill
Russell Mrs. Upway, Hinksey hill
Shorter Geo. 42 Manor rd
Siggars Regnld. 4 St. Lawrence rd
Stockford Mrs. 38 Manor rd
Strong Mrs. 8 Church close
Talbot Kenneth, West Winds, Bettys la
Thomas Wltr. R., M.C. Hillside cott. Hinksey hill
Timms Basil, 40 Manor rd
Titterington Mrs. E. E. B. Bagley cott. Spring copse
Tombs Mrs. F. E. The Firs, Hinksey hill
Trinder Christphr. 5 Church close
Uzzell Norman, 5 Manor rd
Vincent Ewart A., M.A., D.Phil., F.R.I.C. 1 Manor rd
Wager Lawrence R., M.A., D.Sc., F.R.S. 7 Manor rd
Walton E. 18 Manor rd
Waterhouse Mrs. N. Overshot, Badgers la
Wiblin Edwin G. W. A., Hazlewood, Spring copse

Wilkins Edgar, 9 St. Lawrence rd
Willis Jn. B.Sc., Ph.D. Craigellachie, Hinksey hill
Willoughby-Osborne Mrs. A. Woodend, Hinksey hill

COMMERCIAL.

Ambridge Percy J. smallhldr. 23 Manor rd
Austin J. shopfitter, 5 Manor rd
Bayliss Raymond, poultry farmer, The Bungalow, Manor rd

CROSS KEYS P.H.
(M. E. Walker),
16 Manor road. Telephone, Oxford 35407

Flower Wm. farmer, The Lawn, Hinksey hill
General Elliott P.H. 37 Manor rd
Haynes Jn. J. smallholder, Ann Kendal's farm
Howkins Jn. smallholder, Manor farm
Oxford Sports Club (Jn. Thornton, sec. ; Jas. Charlett, steward), Southern By-pass
Parker G. E. (Mrs.), shopkpr. 17 Manor rd
Phillips John (Oxford) Ltd. agricltrl. seedsmen, St. Lawrence rd
South Ward Allotments Association (H. King, sec.), Southern By-pass rd

Kellys Directory 1960 (by permission of Reed Information Service).

The Baptist Chapel, seen here in 1954, before the invasion of telegraph poles and overhead wires. The Chapel was built in 1914 and two commemoration stones, dated 26 February 1914, are on the front of the building, one laid by M R R Alden and one by Mr J Braithwaite. The building is now used as the Village Hall. A short track on the right-hand side leads to a field called 'Paddocks', earlier known as Ringcroft. This field was used for Fetes, including the 1937 Coronation celebration.

Further down Manor Road, with the village shop on the right-hand side. This was known as Parkers or just The Store. During the 1930s the corner house on the left was a shop owned by a Mr Gregory. The Cross Keys public house can be seen in the middle distance. *'The green door bore in glistening brass the number '17' and under it, also in gleaming brass and very larger lettering, the single word 'Parker'. I peeped through the tiny window at what was obviously the village general stores, then the door opened and the great man, George Parker, appeared and courteously beckoned us in. From the moment I set eyes on him I realised that I was in the presence of a real character. As we walked along a dark and narrow corridor he pointed to trophies hanging on the wall, so fast that I hadn't time to see a tenth of them. There was a German Iron Cross, a water-bottle used in the Boer War, Chinese chopsticks, the scarlet pennon of the 21st Lancers, a cannon ball from Chalgrove Field, coins dating back to Roman times, a breast plough, relics of the Indian Mutiny, relics of the Easter Rebellion in Dublin and of the Black and Tans.'*

...he Stores, on the right-hand side, owned and occupied by the Parker family for many ...ars. George Parker had been a member of the Parish Council, known as the Parish ...eeting, for over 25 years. The cottage on the left was occupied by the Keen family in ...e 1950s. The property is now one dwelling.

...n outing from the Cross Keys c.1949. Left to right across back row: Mrs Siggars, ...arcia Walton, Ern Walton, Gert Parslow, Ern Parslow, Mrs Hill, Teddy Hill, George ...rker, Mrs Couling, −, Wendy Litton, Mrs Gladys Parker, Mr Wilkins, −, Mrs ...ilkins, −, Mrs Amos, Evelyn Amos, −, Hazel Harvey, Mr Albert Allsworth, Pearl ...lsworth, Mr Litton. Four children in front: John Hill, −, −, David Parslow.

View from John Piers Lane c.1920 looking towards The Stores in the distance. The lane commemorates John Piers, Archbishop of York from 1589 to 1595, son of a yeoman farmer, who was reputedly born here in 1523. The large house on the right had disappeared by 1968. One of the cottages opposite used to be the school room. These cottages were occupied at one time by the Smith and Keen families.

Mrs Nellie Charlett, wife of Peter Britford Charlett, outside her picturesque cottage, Belle Vue, No. 6 St Lawrence's Road, South Hinksey in 1954. This property is now called The Old Bakehouse although the entrance to the oven is actually next door.

South Hinksey church taken from St Lawrence's Road.

The church of St Laurence is a building of stone, partly of the 13th and partly of the 14th century, consisting of chancel, nave, north porch and a western tower, with plain parapet, containing three bells, two of which are cracked; the nave has a good plain open-timbered roof; the chancel, rebuilt in the 17th century, is divided from the nave by a small and low arch, not more than 6 feet 5 inches in width and there are traces of a rood loft, the stairs to which still remain; the chancel windows were altered and enlarged early in the 18th century; in the south wall is a curious double piscina, and there is one memorial window; the church affords 120 sittings. In the churchyard are the remains of a cross, presumably of the 15th century.

The living is a vicarage, net yearly value £50, with 16 acres of glebe and residence in the gift of the Earl of Abingdon, and held since 1891 by the Reverend William Dixon Blachford Curry MA of Exeter College, Oxford who resides at New Hinksey. The living originally belonged to the Abbey of Abingdon, afterwards it became a chapelry of Cumnor, from which it was separated about 1750, and was subsequently annexed, until 1885, to the vicarage of Wootton. (Extracted from Kellys Directory, 1902.)

Floods in December 1954. 'There was a plaque in the wall opposite the old sweet shop which marks the extent of these floods. It is high off the pavement and the water went swirling round the corner and down John Piers Lane.' (Crozier)

Manor Road c.1930s. Cyril Chandler and his wife lived in the cottage on the left, and Nan Chandler lived in the annexe building behind. On the right are two cottages known as Derwent Cottages. The Stockford family occupied the one on the right-hand side and Harry and Louisa Walton lived in the next. The property was converted in the early 1940s to one dwelling, now known as Stonecroft.

Harry Walton, a carter, and his wife Louisa, probably taken in the garden of Derwent Cottages c.1938. They moved into a small cottage close by, built especially for them. The Stockford family, in the cottage next door, moved to the Council Cottages near the General Eliott. Henry Walton used to work for Old Man Brown on his market garden and 'used to wash the water cress in the stream'.

The Southern By-pass was a two-lane road from the foot of Hinksey Hill to Botley and was promptly nicknamed 'The Road from Nowhere to Nowhere'. During the war it was used as a store for military vehicles and the by-pass was closed at both ends, near South and North Hinksey, for tank assembly. Official passes were required to be carried by the residents of South Hinksey, giving them permission to enter the village.

Oxford City Council reported on 21 January 1930: that land forming part of Raleigh Park, Harcourt Green, land at present leased to Miss Toynbee, the Small Holdings Estate, Barleycote, and Ann Kendall's land be conveyed to the Berkshire County Council for the formation of the by-pass road connecting North and South Hinksey on the following terms, subject to the consent of the Minister of Agriculture and Fisheries and Minister of Health where necessary. Berkshire County Council to compensate the tenants and to fence the land as the road is built. Severence of about 1.88 acres of the Small Holdings Estate to the north of the road and the reduction thereby of its rental value as a Small Holding, a contribution at the rate of 10/- per foot frontage only be made in respect of the land on the north side of the road (approx 970 feet). A contribution at a rate of 10/- per foot frontage only be made in respect of the land on the south side of the road, part of Barleycote and Ann Kendall's land (approx 680 ft) which also has access to the existing Hinksey Road.

Parker Road was constructed when the A34 was made a dual carriageway in 1973 and is named after George Parker of the village.

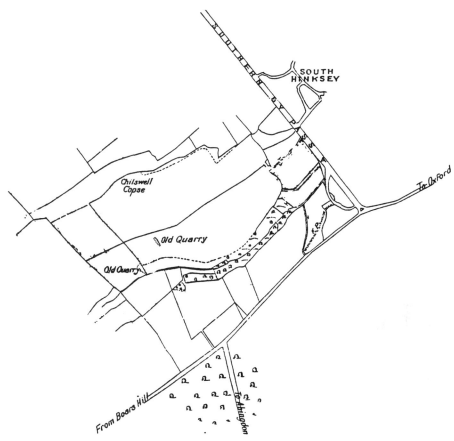

The parish of South Hinksey is still extensive, and includes Hinksey Hill and many surrounding fields and previous smallholdings. The Southern By-pass effectively split it in two and isolated the village from the rest of the parish.

On the opposite side of the Southern By-pass is Chilswell Path, seen here in the 1930s. On both sides of Chilswell Path were common fields belonging to the parish, which were gradually sold to private individuals and businesses.

Jenny Buntings Parlour was a quarry from which stone was dug for the building of All
Souls College, a pretty glen with a tiny stream ending in a copse. This valley has been
used as a rifle range for City Volunteers and therefore closed to the public. (Taunt
c.1917.)

Jenny Bunting was supposedly a young girl in the 17th century who was betrayed in
love and in later years became demented and a recluse in a small hut in the old stone
quarry of the Chilswell Hills. This sad tale is well told in a modern poem written by Mr
Phillipson of South Hinksey, who is particulary interested in the history of the area.

South combe, quarry, trickling stream
Is this a place where lovers dream?
South combe, quarry, place for hunting,
Twas once the home of Jenny Bunting.

Jennie Bunting, who is she pray?
Was born in Yarnton, Peg Broadway.
Dorset bound went widower dad,
Peg aged fifteen, abandoned, sad.

Maid to Clayton she became,
Warden Clayton of Merton fame.
In time a Yorkshire lad she flirted,
She stole for him, he then deserted.

Forced to flee, nought in hand,
She joined in with a gipsy band.
From years of travel far and wide
She entered South combe there to hide.

Pegs she made and pegs she sold,
Total number still untold.
Not for her delights of punting,
The crazy, ageing, Jenny Bunting.

Jenny's ghost now haunts the quarry,
Tho' lovers have no need to worry.
She blesses those whose vows are meant
And curses all with bad intent.

February 1988

Good Friday on Chilswell Hills in 1929, celebrated with donkey rides, games and ice cream. This custom, sometimes referred to as The Custom, seems to have died out after the war. *'Jack Smith, called 'Co-Kee', had a paddock down the end of John Piers Lane. Every year he took his horse and cart up Chilswell Hill on Good Fridays, with pretty coloured balls filled with sawdust on the end of elastic, and coconuts — hence his name of 'Co-Kee'. The Haines family used to give us boys a ½d ice-cream each to help push the three-wheeler trikes up the hill.'*

This photograph of 1927 indicates that 'The Custom' was a big event in the annual calendar, attracting large crowds. The day often ended with youngsters setting light to nearby reed beds.

Henry Taunt in 1917 comments *'Good Friday was a day on which it was more generally fine than wet around Oxford and this seems to be a remnant of a long standing custom of centuries ago, when a calvary was said to have been set up there. Now there are only remains of the fair. Childswell (or Chilswell) was a favourite spot for females wishing for children, to offer up prayers for the desired boon. This may be why it is called Happy Valley, the valley and wood is said to resemble that at Waterloo, but on a much smaller scale'.*

A photograph c.1939 in Jack Howkins field opposite Jo Brown's yard. Jack Howkins sold his produce from a shop on the Abingdon Road. Left to right: Tony Allsworth, John Allsworth, Roy Chandler.

VJ party celebrations in the village. Left to right: Maurice Shorter, Joy Keen, Marcia Walton, Rita Bowler, Tony Gibbons. In front: Tony Allsworth.

Left to right: Roy Chandler, —, Tony Gibbons, Aubrey Gibbons, Ruth Crozier, Betty Parker, and Marcia Walton with shield, —.

View of Manor Road showing Stonecroft on the right and the Chandler residence on the left.

A view from outside The Stores down St Lawrence's Road c.1910. The Cross Keys public house is on the right-hand side. The landlord at this time was 'Bodger' Davis who also ran the blacksmith's shop on the opposite side of the road behind the trees. This property is now known as the Donkey House. On the same side of the road are three cottages; the nearest one was School Cottage.

Coach outing from the vilage c.1950. Left to right front row: Stanley Howkins, Frank Hulbert, Pat 'Sugar' Strange, Susan Hulbert, Jenny Harvey, Ann Howkins, Brian Howkins, Ray Uzzell, Norman Uzzell, Michael Uzzell, Fred Regan, Pat Regan. Back row: Clive Allsworth, Lew Howkins, David Strange, Maud Harvey, Daphne Hulbert, Florence Allsworth, Janet Allsworth, Gordon Eadle, Albert Allsworth, Sylvia Uzzell, Chris Hulbert, Florence Uzzell, Derek Strange, Reg Howkins, Olive Howkins, Lil Strange, –.

Janet Allsworth at a village celebration during the Festival of Britain in 1951.

New Hinksey School

New Hinksey Girls 1920–21. Left to right back row: Edna Shelton, Joan Fowler, Edna Pitt, Ivy Wallace, — Brakespear, Vera Temple, Phyll Green, Doris Lee, Hilda Adams. Next row, half hidden: Ruby Siggars, Nora Siggars, —, —, Nora Knott, Emily Carter, Freda Adams, Ethel Simmons, — Chandler. Next row: Gladys Walker, Rene Shelton, Madge Clanville, Trixie Grundy, Tiny Williams, Gladys Nutt, Clara Nott, Sue Smith, Edith Webb, — Chandler. Front row: Nora Trinder, Leta Loyn, Rose Honey, Vera Wheeler, Nancy Coles, Mollie Stimpson, Edna Pledge, — Tombs, Dolly Bull.

New Hinksey School was built in 1870, enlarged in 1892 and again in 1899, for 178 boys, 155 girls and 170 infants; the average attendance was 128 boys, 128 girls, 112 infants. In 1902 Joseph Sydney Thomas was master, Miss F Collins, mistress and Miss R Penn infants mistress. *'Headmaster was at one time 'Gaffer' Thomas. Thomas was a stickler, us kids had to be careful. Other teachers I remember were Mrs Stewart and Miss Louie Harding — she was a very good teacher — stood no nonsense but could control any hooligan — Mr Jones and Miss Room. At that time the boys' school was nearest to Stewart Street and the girls' next to Church Lane. It was later a mixed school. An honours board used to hang at New Hinksey school recording the names and dates of all scholarships, but this has now vanished.'* (Harold)

'When the art teacher, Miss Harding, died we all took 6d to school to buy a lamp which still hangs in the church today.'

New Hinksey school c.1925 Std I. Left to right standing against back wall: Nellie Timms, Bill Phillips, –, Fred Honey, –, –. Standing against side wall, from front: –, – –, – McKenzie. Left to right front row: –, –, – Allen?, –, –. Second row: –, –, Ethany Woodidge, Maudie Binder, – Pitts. Third row: –, –, –, Ruby Purvey, –. Fourth row: – Bill Church, Eddie Thomas, –, Wally King. Fifth row: –, –, –, Ray Higgs, –.

New Hinksey Boys School c.1927. Left to right back row: –, Eddie Thomas, Joe Jessett –, Eric Grundy, Gordon Ayres, Ray Higgs. Next row: Donald McKenzie, – Cox, – Derek Stacy, Eric Bowles, Cyril Pitt, Wally King, Alec Messenger. Next row: – Hill, –, –, –, –, Dick Simmonds, Fred Honey, Frank Brewster. Front row: – Juggins – Fowles, Billy Church, –, Bill Phillips, –.

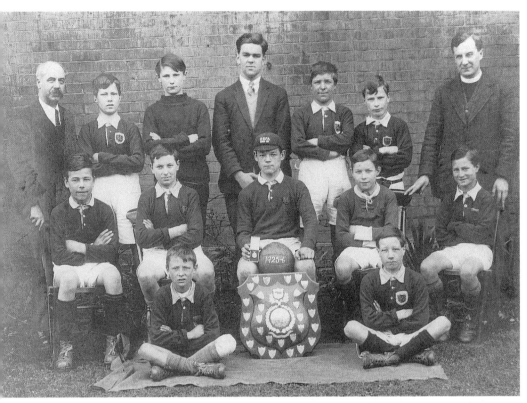

New Hinksey School Football XI 1925/6, winners of the Oxford Elementary Schools FA Senior Shield. Left to right back row: 'Gaffer' Thomas, L Strange, George Moles, Colin King, B Sherman, A Harris, Reverend J W C Moore. Middle row: F Pursey, W Ilsley, W Reade (capt.), Bill Varney, George Harris. In front: W Owen, Gordon McKenzie.

New Hinksey Girls Country Dancing Shield. Left to right back row: −, −, Miss Stone teacher, −, −, −. Front row: −, −, Betty Stimpson, Vera Blackgrove. Miss Stone lived on the Abingdon Road, next to Rev. Stather-Hunt who occupied 118 Abingdon Road, which was St Matthews Vicarage.

New Hinksey Girls Class I c.1926. The group includes May Blake, Elsie Pitts, Nancy Coles, Lena Rawlings, Florrie Harvey, Vera Wheeler. Standing: Francis Bowerman, Irene Shelton, Alice Hayward, Gwen Edens, Rose Honey. Other girls in this year were Eva Owen, Phyllis Waters, Gertie Parsons, Amy Lee, Mary Wigmore, Vera Revell, Trixie Grundy, Joan Taylor. The head teacher at this time was Miss Penn who lived in Norreys Avenue.

New Hinksey School Football 1928. Left to right back row: Walter Woodidge, −, −, − Prestidge, Colin King, −, Charles Lynes. Middle row: −, Arthur Temple, George Shelton, Den Sandalls, −. Front row: Len Shelton, − Fowles, − McKenzie.

New Hinksey School Senior Shield 1927/8. Left to right back row: Mr Thomas headmaster, —, — Prestidge, Colin King, —, G Emburgh, Reverend Moore. Middle row: Stan Hicks, — Cudd, Billy Read, P Harris, T Dunkley. Front row: Jack Adams, —.

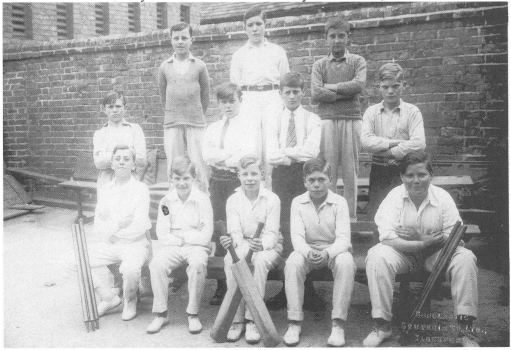

New Hinksey School Cricket XI c.1925/6. Left to right back row: Ron Garrett, Jack Adams, Jack Franklin. Middle row: Henry Adams, Chris Trinder, Len Prestidge, Taffy Stoke. Front row: Les Bonner whose family sold fruit and veg in the covered market in Oxford, John Chance, Frank Adams, Ted Heath, Roly Relf.

New Hinksey Boys c.1928. Left to right back row: −, −, Joe Jessett, −, Norman Bowley, − Aldridge, − McKenzie, −, Bill Church. Next row: −, −, − Hill, − Gray, − Kitchen, − Juggins, −, Peter Best. Next row: −, Cyril Pitt, Wally King, Edwin Thomas, Frank Brewster, Derek Stacy, Laurie Church, −, Len Shelton. Next row: Dick Simmonds, Bill Phillips, Bob Warne, −, Phil Crozier, Donald McKenzie, Eric Bowles, −. Front row: Dennis Mace, Charlie Marshall, Dave Cox, Eric Grundy, Jim Fowles, Frank Samuels.

New Hinksey Football Team c.1932. Mr Bodenham at back. Next row left to right: − Underwood, Bill Phillips, Ray Higgs, Maurice Varney, − Lester. Next row: Chick Sawyer, Victor Cross, Dick Simmons, Dennis Mace, Alf Jefferies. Front: Norman Shelton, − Hornblow.

New Hinksey Std VI c.1937. Left to right front row: Daphne Downer, Colin Belcher, —, Gordon Skuce, —, —, —, —. Second row: all unknown. Third row: —, Betty Parker, Denis Taylor, rest unknown. Fourth row: —, Peter Keen, rest unknown. Back row: —, Aubrey Gibbons, —, —, —, —, Eric Shelton, rest unknown.

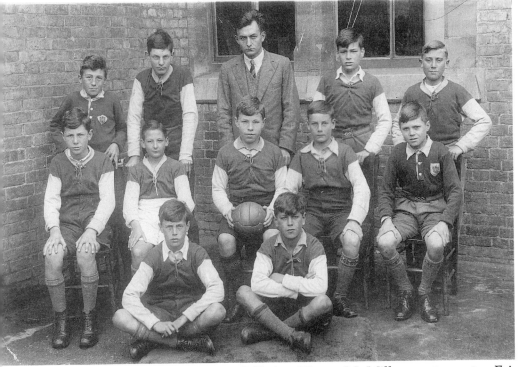

Football team 1934 includes Alf 'Ginger' Jefferies, S Long, Mr Miller sports master, Eric Bowles, — Hughes, — Hewer, Len Shelton, — Kitching, — Mace, Den Franklyn, Dick Simmons.

Football team 1936/37, senior side. Left to right back row: Mr White headmaster, - Brooks, - Parkinson, Reverend Lander, - Wigmore, Sam Pitts, Mr Billingham. Middl(row: Ron Jefferies, Ralph Smith, Dennis Bowles, L Revell, C Collins. Front row: Bol Simmonds, 'Son' Bowler.

'I remember Edie Foster, a girl of about 9 years old; she was a handful. Soon afte Mr Billingham came to the school, I remember, he had longish blond wavey hair an she pulled it. He made her stand outside the door and soon the class heard a smal voice through the door 'Who's afraid of the big bad wolf'. But we didn't dare laugh.'

An extract from South Hinksey Parish Magazine 1929.
Sunday Schools: A service was held in Church on Sunday afternoon, March 10th, when prizes were given for regular attendance during the past year. Forty-five young people received books, these having obtained at least 90 per cent full marks.

We are hoping this year to take into consideration not only regular attendance, but also conduct, both in Church and Sunday School.

The following are the names of those who received prizes:-
Girls:
Class 1: J Blagrove, A Day, V Greenwood, V Temple, A Walker
Class 2: D Arkell, G Brown, F Snelgrove, H Arkell, J Fowler, B Lynes, V Blagrove
Class 3: L Keen, N Hickmott, G Pitt, D Dingle, K Hawkes
Class 4: J Aspell, G Hayward, P Parker, M Franklin, D Pitts, G Giles
Boys:
Class 1: F Adams, R Greenwood, J Mackenzie, G Franklin, G Barrett, E Skuce
Class 2: R Keen, F Thomas, R Garrett, C Wheeler, W Lynes
Class 3: W Souch, A Pitts, L Aspell, E Haines, L Belcher, C Warne, C Lynes
Class 4: W Woodage, W Franklin, N Bowley, A Bowley.

Cold Arbour

On the right of the photograph, c.1895, are the Salthouses, single storey houses built during the early nineteenth century. Raised planks were positioned on bricks along this section of the Abingdon Road for pedestrians and cyclists. The milestone situated outside the nearest house still remains in Abingdon Road. The brick wall on the right is the boundary of the city's Infectious Diseases Hospital, built in 1886. The white building in the middle distance is Cold Arbour House, now part of the Fox and Hounds public house, which was rebuilt in 1926.

Extract from St Matthews Parish Magasine, November 1894: *'The all-engrossing topic of conversation and matter for thought during the month has been the floods. Thousands have visited Grandpont and the other districts affected, mostly impelled by curiosity, yet much sympathy has been aroused and not a little pecuniary help forthcoming, the Central Fund reaching £250. We may take comfort from the fact that it is some fifty years since a similar inundation and hope it may be longer still before we have another. To visit Cold Arbour (the name might well have been Harbour) in a lorry, and to be obliged to get bread and coal through the upper windows, was a novel experience.'* The area has indeed become known as Cold Harbour, possibly a reflection of the regular floods, which are still experienced today.

Cold Arbour, on the Abingdon Road, was part of St Aldate's parish in 1902, becoming part of St Matthews when Grandpont became a separate parish in 1913. This view o 1895 shows Cold Arbour House on the left looking towards the Salt Boxes. *'Cold Arbour means 'shelter from the cold', a place to rest after a long journey. Originally a hamlet situated at the junction of Abingdon Road and Weirs Lane in early 1800s Mentioned in 1822–3 and c.1840.'* (Marriott)

An outing from the Fox and Hounds public house in the early 1930s. Left to right back row: Jack Hedges, Arthur Cotterell, −, Mr Mitchell, Mr Jefferies, −, Mr Moodey, Mr Savins, −. Middle row: Mr Waite, −, Mr Kingham, three unknown, Mr Clapton, Bill Ilsley. Front row: Mr Charlie Honour, Mr Eatwell, −, −, Edmund Ilsley landlord, −, −, Mr Wakelin. The Fox and Hounds at 279 Abingdon Road is a large fake Tudoresque timber house on the corner of Donnington Bridge Road. The first inn was mentioned in 1871 and was on the site of the present petrol station next door in Abingdon Road.

The Farriers' Arms, Abingdon Road in 1946.

Originally built as a private house in 1776, it was named the Further White House to distinguish it from the White House closer to Folly Bridge. By 1779 it was a hospital for smallpox victims and was run by Mary Elliss. Here, it was claimed, Bristow, a surgeon from Cassington, and a certain Freeman Tripp experimented with inoculation.

In 1885 the hospital, then known as the City Isolation Hospital, moved across the road and continued to provide isolation facilities for smallpox, scarlet fever, diphtheria, scabies, whooping cough and tuberculosis until 1939 when a new hospital was opened at the Slade, Headington. The old hospital and grounds became the Rivermead Rehabilitation Hospital specialising in the treatment of young disabled patients.

In 1872 the original pioneering hospital became the Farrier's Arms after a farrier at Cold Arbour. Two licensees are recorded during this period, Tom Morgan in 1872 and Jason Buckett in 1880. The licensee in 1902 was Alfred Revell. Mr and Mrs Frank Ayres held the license during the 1930s and 1940s, later held by their son, Gordon and his wife Meriel. It was very small with only two floors, a front porch and central room with bars either side. Modernised in 1930, it was closed in May 1963 and used as an office for the County Surveyor during the building of the Oxford by-pass. Shortly afterwards, it was pulled down to make way for the spur road to that by-pass.

Oxford City Council Minutes 3 June 1930: that Mr A J Smith of 43 Sunningwell Road be offered the tenancy of a quarter of an acre of land adjoining the Farriers' Arms for the purpose of storing his stock-in-trade and tools as a painter and decorator at a rental of £20 per annum, subject to six months notice on either side.

A coach outing from The Farriers' Arms c1937. Left to right back row: Mrs Diamond, Mrs Tottenham, Mrs Roberts, Mrs Ayres landlady, Mrs Bull, Edna Roberts, –, Mrs Wheeler, Mrs Jefferies, Mrs Stewart, Mrs Lil Haines, –. The lady on the coach steps is Mrs Rona Rawlings. Front row: Mrs Butler, Mrs Smith, Mrs Florrie Bowler of Canning Crescent, Mrs Florrie Bowler of Weirs Lane, –, Mrs Kent, Gladys Finch, Mrs Cannon, Mrs Rose Theobold, Mrs Jessett, Alice Finch, –. Mrs Lil Haines was a member of the Haines family whose rag and bone business was situated where the Kennington gipsy site is now. They lived in Cold Arbour, behind the Fox and Hounds.

Rivermead Hospital.

A fever hospital was constructed at Cold Arbour in 1883. This was due to St John's College refusing to renew the lease on the site of the Old Fever Hospital, built 1871, in the Woodstock Road. The original two-ward hospital was enlarged in 1894 to take fever patients who had earlier been treated at the Radcliffe Infirmary and Cowley Road Workhouse hospitals. A new isolation hospital, the Slade, opened in Headington in 1939 but the Cold Arbour hospital continued to be used as an extra hospital throughout World War II. In 1955 it reopened as a rehabilitation hospital for the chronic sick and elderly and in 1960 it became a general rehabilitation centre with new workshops and physiotherapy facilities.

The Abingdon Road, at the top of Pitt Road, now Chatham Road, and Weirs Lane during the floods of 1947. The shops on the left-hand side used to be a grocers, Lynches, at No. 334, and Brooks & Belcher, confectioners, at Nos. 328 and 330.

The South Oxford Garage on the left-hand side still exists as a garage at the top of Monmouth Road. The proprietor at this time was A T Baskerville who used to live in nearby Northampton Road; his house was called Bask Villa. On the other side of Northampton Road was a shop belonging to Harry Wiggins, a corn merchant. to the left of the garage, out of sight, is a property called Green Gables. This was a surgery for many years for Dr Arthur Stevens, later Drs James Blackman and Strode.

A photograph believed to be c.1965. The railway line is at the bottom of the picture with the Red Bridge on the right. The Rivermead Hospital complex is top right.

Aerial photograph of Cold Arbour looking south with Abingdon Road on the left.

New council houses near completion in Weirs Lane in the 1920s. These houses were
being built on land that the City Council had bought from University College. On the
right, the house with an almost flat roof was one of a pair of paper houses built in the
nineteenth century for workers at the nearby Weirs paper mill. Council housing on the
south side of Weirs Lane replaced the old paper houses in about 1930. The lane led
down to Weirs Mill, and it remained a cul-de-sac for vehicles until Donnington Bridge
was completed in November 1962.

   'Before the housing estate was built on the Coldarbour fields over sixty years ago
Weirs Lane was a narrow country lane. It led on to the footbridge over the weirs on the
loop of river which rejoins the main river at Kennington. From there the path went
over the fields to the towing path, as it still does. There was no bridge over the Thames
to Donnington then, so pedestrians wishing to go to Iffley road were ferried across by
punt. Later, a high footbridge was built and much more recently the present road
bridge.

   Coldarbour fields always flooded in the winter so the ground was raised above
flood level with household rubbish. I remember the open topped rubbish carts going
down Abingdon Road and tipping their contents on the fields.

   In those days Coldarbour was just a few houses, a pub and the Isolation Hospital
which is now Rivermead Rehabilitation Centre.

   The new housing estate was, and is, in St Matthews parish. So funds were soon
being raised to build a mission church in Canning Crescent to serve the new
community. It is now more than fifty years since St Luke's was built and it is hard to
realise that the houses and the church have not always been there.' (St Matthews Parish
Centre)

   Oxford City Council Minutes 6 May 1930: that the Reverend D K Stather-Hunt be
granted a lease of vacant land with a frontage of approximately 77 feet to Canning
Crescent and a depth of 87 feet for a period of twenty-one years at a ground rent of £20
per annum.

The Old 'Uns played the Young 'Uns at football soon after 1939 on a field near the Weirs. The photograph includes Bert Archer, — Randall, George Whip, — Clapton.

George V Silver Jubilee party 1935 in the Recreation Ground off Fox Crescent. The photograph includes Mrs Buckell, Edna Roberts, George Bowler, Bert Bowler, Florrie Bowler, Peggie Bowler, Mrs Atkinson, Mrs Wheeler, Reverend Stather-Hunt, Norman Stewart, Mr Goodgame, Fred Taylor, May Taylor, Reverend Phillips, Fred Butler, Mr Chandler. The local Mums had dressed up as 'nippies from Lyons', the waiting staff from the tea shop in Oxford City Centre, while they waited on the children.

A street party in Fox Crescent held in September 1951 to commemorate the Festival of Britain. Five year old Christine Archer, at the head of the table, was crowned Festival Queen by the Reverend Chamberlain. Included in the photograph are Mrs Archer, Mick Stockford, Robin Norris, Alan Cox, Mavis Smith, Shirley Scragg, Joan Scragg, Doreen Harris, Rosemary Lewis, Teddy Lewis, Mrs Dyer, Mrs Witts.

Cold Arbour Football Club members 1934/35: Left to right back row: A Foster, Bill Breakspear, Fred Taylor, Tom Hillier, Bill Dean, W Collett. Next row: A Kingham Hon Secretary, Percy Harris, Bill Boswell, C Mack, Harry Moody, Frank Ledwell, Arthur Drage, A Lynch Hon. Treasurer. Next row: Gilbert Bray, Stan Honour, Oliver Horn, George Honour, Fred Butler, Bill Timms, R Wall, Ron Goodgame. Front row: Ted Boswell, Peter Smith, J Diamond, — Smith (mascot), Peter Maskell, W Moody.

old Arbour Senior League 1970/71 season: Left to right back row: Gordon Harris
anager, Paul Dawson, Maurice East, –, Mike Griffiths, Jimmy Rawlings, Pat Souch,
- Cooke, Doug Califano Hon. Secretary. Front row: Michael Collins, Eddie Knevett,
ean McKiernan, Bruce Bennett, Brian Clapton, Norman Brown, Peter Williams. This
hotograph was taken at the White House Grounds. The team usually played on
ldens Meadows and, before the war, on Turners field in Cold Arbour.

Cold Arbour Sunday League 1975. Back row: Bill Breakspear manager, Tommy Eales,
rnie Cranford, Dave Nightingale, Michael Collins, John Bailey, Terry Jeakins, David
'ill. Front row: Steve James, John Pagano, Adie Rippington, Brian Thorne, Les Buckett,
'ony Tompkins.

CANNING CRESCENT
from 32 Weir's lane to
Abingdon road.

EAST SIDE.
1 Kent Wm
3 Lord Ernest
5 Jefferies Alfd. Jn
7 Hollis Harry
9 Taylor Fredk
11 Treadwell Miss J
13 Whittaker Thos
15 Harris Geo. Fredk
17 Holt Percy Fredk
19 Savins Mrs. Mary
23 Watkins Thos. Godfrey
25 Messenger Geo
27 Davies Jas. I
29 Parrott Wm. Regnld
31 Archer Alfd
33 Liley Albt. Edwd

35 Finch Wm. Chas
37 Yates Alfd. Cyril
39 Bannister Amos
41 Rawlings Hy
43 Haynes Fredk
45 Aldridge Sidney
47 Oliver Percy

WEST SIDE.
2 Bowler Albt
4 Haynes Jn. Jas
6 Roberts Mrs
8 Grainger Percvl
10 Skelcher Ben
12 Curtis Arth. Hy
14 Drage Ernest Geo
16 Caunon Wm. Jn
18 Goodgame Mrs. E. S
20 Heredge Wm. Job
22 Roberts Thos
24 Skelcher Danl
26 Burling Ernest
28 Preston Fredk. Geo
30 Luker Mrs. S. A
32 Slaymaker Albt
34 Weaving Jesse
36 Ward Mrs
ST. LUKE'S CHURCH

COLD ARBOUR (New
Hinksey), from Abingdon
road to City boundary.

EAST SIDE.

..... here is Weirs la ......

Fox & HoundsP.H.Edmund
Ilsley
Ilsley Edmnd. & Son,
coal mers
Robinson Christopher(Cold
Arbour house)

COLD ARBOUR PLACE:

1 Pickett Arth. Jn
2 Viner Arthur
3 Merry Spencer
4 Bennett Geo. Edwin

Ilsley Edmnd. & Son, coal
& coke mers

... here is Canning cres ...

OxfordCorporationHospital
for Infectious Diseases
(for full particulars of
staff see entry in Official
section)

Mitchell Saml.(The Lodge)
Ayres Frank, beer retlr
Middleton Geo. Edwd.
(Red cott)
Cox Mrs. F. (The Haven)
Revell Alfd. H. butcher

WEST SIDE.

356 Goodchild Norman W
358 Day Ernest Wm
360 Wakelin Redvers Cecil
362 White Mrs. E
364 Lloyd Herbt. Canning
366 Smith Hy. Eric
368 Webb Archie A
370 Wiggins Wm. Fras
372 Long Jas

374 Smith Percvl. Arth.
chimney sweep
376 Butler Geo. Hy
378 Breakspear Wltr. C
380 Ramsey Jsph. Hy
382 Young Fredk
384 Cross Sidney
386 Bustin Herbt
388 Stafford Rt
390 Ledwell Frank Jn
392 Wheeler Harold
394 Woodley Mrs. D
396 Claydon Mrs. E
398 Smith Fredk. Wm
400 Walton Edwd
402 Cox Miss R
404 Eustace Mrs. H
406 Butler Mrs. S. A
408 Woodward Geo
410 Smith Frank B
412 Sparrow Cecil Jn
414A, Hedges Mrs. S

...... here is Bertie pl ......

416 Tyrrell Mrs
416A, Smith Mrs. E
418 Buckett Jn. Stanley
420 Strange Archie
422 Gibbons Geo
Redbridge Garage
(A. Burton, propr)
Timms Wm. Wltr.
(Bridge cott)
Drewett Mrs. (Rose
cott)
Drewet Bertie J.
house painter (Rose
cott)

PITT ROAD (St.Aldate's),
from 261 Abingdon road to
Fox crescent.

NORTH SIDE.
1 Waite Wallace
3 Busson Alfd. B
5 Stacey William Albert
7 Pointer John
9 Wakefield Fredk
11 Hurst Arth
13 Baldwin Jesse
15 Trinder Jack
17 Hall Sidney Geo
19 Young Arth. Jas
21 Cox Raymond
23 Hill Thos. G
25 Sadler Chas
27 Hedges William
29 Boswell Mrs. E
31 Davis Ernest Albert
33 Gillard Mrs. F. C
35 Coombes Wltr. Edgar
37 Saunders Richard Wm
39 Richings Eric Arth. J
41 Haines James Alfred
43 Diamond Herbert John

SOUTH SIDE.
2 Hillier Thos. Hy
4 Talboys Percy
6 Merry Ernest
8 Kingham Albt. Jn
10 Wilkins Jn. Hy
12 Hodges Chas. Edwd
14 Collett Wm
16 Simmonds Wm. Geo
18 Underwood Archbld. M
20 Gardner Fredk. Geo
22 Moody Mrs. Fanny
24 Maisey Jn. Regnld
26 Wyatt Albt
28 King Geo
30 Butcher Chas. A
32 Bowles Charles
34 Humphries Almeric E
36 Waine Walter John
38 Turner Fredk. Walter
40 Goodwin Lionel
42 Edwards Robert
44 Jeffery Joseph

WEIRS LA. (St. Aldate's),
from 277 Abingdon road.

SOUTH SIDE.
10 Wappner Mrs. A
12 Edney Mrs
14 Spiers Jn. Jas
16 Boswell Mrs

...... here is Peel pl .....

18 Butler Geo
20 Honour Albt
22 Brakespear Wm
24 Finch Wm
26 Marchant Sidney
28 Bazeley Mrs. C. A
30 Stroudley Mrs. R
32 Bowler Geo

... here is Canning cres ...

34 Clapton Jas. Herbt
36 Dyer Ernest Chas
38 Stanmore Mrs. Lizzie,
genl. shop
40 Morris Ernest
42 Dawson Percvl
44 Harris Ernest Edwd.
boat bldr

NORTH SIDE.
1 Horn Henry
3 Hayes Geo. Wm
5 Smith William Thomas
7 Hill Louis
9 Chapman Frank
11 Collins Jn. Louis
13 Atkinson Joseph
15 Wall Wm. Thos
17 Brightman Fredk. Geo
19 Taylor Sidney M
21 Mitchell George Wm
23 Field Wm. Hy
25 Cox Whyburne Hy. G
27 Randall Horace Geo
29 Fidler Albt
31 Pomeroy Chas. Hy
33 Greenway Alfd. Jn
35 Rowland Sidney Chas
37 Dunn Wltr
39 Barratt Fras. Albt
41 Mahoney Jn
43 Baughan Chas. Alfd
...... here is Fox cres ......
45 Hines Hy. Jesse
47 Bailey Frank Ernest
49 Bennett Fredk. Wm
51 Pegler Edward G
53 Tombs Arth
Silverstone Jas. (Weirs
ho)
Harris Ernest Edwd.
boat bldr. (works)

Extract from Kelly's Directory 1937 (by permission of Reed Information Service).

pposite Weirs Lane and Canning Crescent, on the other side of Abingdon Road, is
ertie Place named in 1935 after the Bertie family, Earls of Abingdon 17th–20th
entury. This street party, held for the 1953 Coronation of Queen Elizabeth II, includes:
1rs Washington, David and Jimmy Washington, Mrs Bailey, Mrs Young, John Young,
1rs Smith, Doreen and George Smith, Mr and Mrs Gibbons, Bobby and Jenny Gibbons,
1rs D Smith, Ivy, Beryl and Brenda Smith, Mrs Butler, Eileen, Laurence and Michael
utler, Mrs Dot Young, Mrs Bucket, Pauline Harris, Peter Strange, Gordon Ledwell,
leather Brown, George Dearlove, Susan Hill, Mrs Dawson, Mrs McKernam and
ridget McKernam, Mr Griffith, Freddy Munday, Michael Munday, Charlie Mulley,
1ary Mulley, Richard Goodgame, Mavis and Doris Goodgame, Michael and Elizabeth
eene, Gillian, Morris and Malcolm Routledge, Margery Goodall, Carol Fisher,
Jorman Underwood, Mr Grimshaw.

A party in Fox Crescent held for the Coronation of King George VI in 1937. The group includes, from the left: Peggy Howes, Michael Spiers, Audrey Goodgame, Helen Butcher (Queen of the May, in front), Mary Mulley, Florence Cotterell, Alan Randall (John Bull in front), Margaret Fidler, Bernice Hedges, Phyllis Allsworth, Joan Saunders, Myrtle Wilson, Iris Wilson, James 'Daddy' Haines (old man in hat at the back). 'Daddy Haines was a small man, and always smoked a pipe. When he rode his bike he could barely reach the pedals. He suddenly collapsed and died at the City football grounds in Whitehouse Road, while watching Oxford City play'.